Independence
in
Latin America
A Comparative Approach

STUDIES IN
WORLD CIVILIZATION
*Consulting Editor:*
Eugene Rice
*Columbia University*

# Independence in Latin America

RICHARD GRAHAM
*University of Texas at Austin*

Alfred A. Knopf  *New York*

THIS IS A BORZOI BOOK
PUBLISHED BY ALFRED A. KNOPF, INC.

Copyright © 1972 by Richard Graham
All rights reserved under International and Pan-American
Copyright Conventions. Published in the United States by
Alfred A. Knopf, Inc., New York, and simultaneously in Canada
by Random House of Canada Limited, Toronto. Distributed by
Random House, Inc., New York.

Library of Congress Cataloging in Publication Data
Graham, Richard, 1934–      . Independence in Latin America.
(Studies in world civilization)
Bibliography: p. 133.
1. Latin America—History—Wars of Independence, 1806–1830.
I. Title. II. Series. F1412.G64 980′.02 70–152716
ISBN 0–394–31641–X

Manufactured in the United States of America

First Edition

9 8 7 6 5 4 3 2 1

Typography and cover design by Elton Robinson.

Cover map by J. P. Tremblay.

To My Mother and
the Memory of My Father

# Preface

It is a commonplace that comparative history must deal with comparable phenomena. The student of European history may be misled into thinking that the independence movements in Latin America can be compared to the French Revolution whose stances and phrases were so often mimicked throughout Latin America. To be sure, the independence movements in Latin America were marked by profound changes in world view which undermined the foundations of traditional, corporate society, but the changes were more like those associated with the Renaissance than those identified with social revolution.

The comparisons that will prove most productive are those between and among the various regions and groups of Latin America itself. If this point is to be accepted, the student must first recognize that Latin America is not one undifferentiated whole; such recognition will itself be a major step toward opening up new vistas for the student whose horizons have otherwise been limited by his own cultural heritage. Understanding the variety of an area such as Latin America is a step toward ending the provincialism expressed in the phrase "they all look alike." My purpose, then, is to give the student of European history sufficient depth in a particular area and a particular series of events so that he can begin to see his own tradition from a broader perspective. It is for this reason that, in addition to making broad generalizations about Latin America in an era of change, I explore the diversity of regional and group reaction to that change.

Furthermore, an examination of the process through which the political independence of Latin America was established will lead the reader to a fuller realization of the dynamics of European history. For the rise of industrial capitalism and the resulting European drive to construct a single world economy cannot be fully understood unless seen from the point of view of an underdeveloped region engulfed by the emerging system but having no part in its direction. Although practically every European history textbook refers to the expansion of Europe, it is not the era of discovery and conquest that best exemplifies that process. It may even be argued that it was precisely when the political control of overseas colonies was relatively weak that the process of European expansion was most intense. But in any case, its full meaning can be grasped only from the perspective of the recipient culture.

For the student of Latin American history there has not been, until now, any book-length survey in English of the independence movements in all of Latin America. Even Spanish- and Portuguese-speaking historians have usually been too concerned with their own national histories; and when occasionally these historians have looked beyond the borders of their own countries, they have been circumscribed by those ancient cultural barriers that have long divided Iberian peoples: Brazil is ignored by Spanish-Americans and vice versa.

The reader acquainted with Latin America will note some omissions here that require a word of explanation. The story of independence in Central America, Paraguay, and Ecuador did not appear sufficiently significant for inclusion here; and Haiti's case was too diverse to allow sufficient development within the brief confines of the present study. Finally, I did not find the background and course of the First War of Independence in Colombia sufficiently productive of comparative insights to warrant full discussion. Otherwise, all areas of Latin America receive substantial attention.

I am grateful to Charles C. Griffin, Hugh M. Hamill, and Richard N. Sinkin, who read through earlier versions and gave much helpful advice, and to Eugene Rice, who provided editorial help from start to finish. Special thanks are due to my students on whom I tried out several of these ideas and from whom I gathered many. Both advice and ideas were sometimes ignored, so the end result is entirely my responsibility.

R. G.

March 1971                                    *Austin, Texas*

# Contents

# Introduction

Professor Graham's comparative study of how the principal regions of Latin America won their political independence is one in a series of twelve paperbacks which Alfred A. Knopf, Inc., is publishing under the title *Studies in World Civilization.* A second study will be devoted to colonial Latin America. Of the ten other studies in the series, one book deals with early and one with modern developments in Africa, China, India, Japan, and the Middle East. The purposes of the series are to introduce students early in their careers to the historical experience of peoples, societies, and civilizations different from their own; to provide a core of attractive readings for courses in World Civilization; and to make it easier for teachers of Western Civilization to include in their courses comparative evidence from non-Western history and from the less familiar areas of the Western world.

One of the intellectual virtues of our time is a willingness to recognize both the relativism of our own past and present beliefs and the civilizing value of the study of alien cultures. Yet in practice, as every teaching historian knows, it is immensely difficult to construct a viable course in world history and almost as difficult to include satisfactory unfamiliar, and especially non-Western, materials in the traditional Western Civilization survey course. The reason for this difficulty is that until very recently mankind had no common past. The pre-Columbian civilizations of America attained their splendor in total isolation from the rest of the world. Although the many different ancient peoples living around the Mediterranean were often in close touch with one another, they had little knowledge about civilizations elsewhere. The Chinese knew accurately no other high civilization. Until the nineteenth century, they regarded the ideals of their own culture as normative for the entire world. Medieval Europe, despite fruitful contact with the Islamic world, was a closed society; medieval Western historians identified their own past with the history of the human race and gave it meaning and value by believing that this past was the expression of a providential plan.

The fifteenth-century European voyages of discovery began a new era in the relations between Europe and the rest of the world. Between 1600 and 1900, Europeans displaced the populations of three other continents, conquered India, partitioned Africa, and decisively influenced the historical development of China and Japan. The expansion of Europe over the world gave Western historians a unifying theme: the story of how the non-Western world became the economic hinterland, political satellite, and technological debtor of Europe. Despite an enormously increased knowledge of the religions, arts and literatures, social structures, and political institutions of non-Western peoples, Western historians wrote a universal history that remained radically provincial. Only their assumptions changed. Before 1500, these assumptions were theological; by the nineteenth century, they were indistinguishable from those of intelligent colonial governors.

The decline of European dominance, the rise to power of hitherto peripheral Western countries such as the United States and the Soviet Union and of non-Western ones such as China and Japan, and the emergence of a world economy and a state-system embracing the planet have all created further options and opened wider perspectives. Historians of the future will be able to write real world history because for good and ill the world has begun to live a single history; and while this makes it no easier than before to understand and write the history of the world's remoter past, contemporary realities and urgencies have widened our curiosity, enlarged our sympathies, and made less provincial our notion of what is relevant to us in our historical inheritances.

Two tactics suggest themselves as viable methods for overcoming the ethnocentric provincialism of an exclusively Western perspective. One approach, especially appropriate in dealing with a non-Western civilization, is comparative history. The comparative procedure has a double advantage. On the one hand, it describes a culture different from our own and makes clear to us that in order to understand that culture we must scan its history with humility and sophistication, abandoning implicit analogies with our own civilization and leaving aside some of our most fundamental assumptions about time, space, causality, and even about human nature itself. On the other hand, it encourages us to make explicit those very assumptions of our own tradition we now recognize to be different or unique. By studying comparatively an alien civilization we learn something about that civilization—a good in itself—and at the same time sharpen our understanding of ourselves.

A second approach, more appropriate to the history of areas of the world colonized or settled by Europeans, is to study cultural diffusion: how Europe, in the modern period, exported men, ideas and techniques, to America for example, and how Europeans and Americans attempted to fit them to a new environment and new needs. In this way too we sharpen our awareness of what is distinctive both in the European past and in those societies of European origin transplanted to other continents.

Professor Graham's penetrating essay on the establishment of political independence in Latin America exploits both these tactics. His book is an admirable introduction to a seminal and dramatic period in Latin American history. Professor Graham consciously designed it to be read also in the larger perspectives of Western and world history. One of his major themes is the accelerating "Europeanization" of Latin America between 1700 and 1900, for he rightly believes that the dynamic expansionism of European culture can be understood adequately only by studying its impact on a recipient culture. The other problems of modern Latin American history he selects for emphasis are at the same time the fundamental problems of modern world history: revolt, revolution, and coup d'état; wars of aggression and of liberation; national aspiration and nationalist passion; colonialism and the struggle to escape it; racial antagonism; capitalism and poverty. The comparative evidence from Latin America assembled here by Professor Graham will complement similar evidence from other continents and enrich the discussion of modernization in whatever part of the world the historian chooses to investigate it.

EUGENE RICE
*Columbia University*

# Independence
# in
# Latin America
## A Comparative Approach

# Chapter 1

# A Century
of Change

Two trends characterize the history of all Latin America between the eighteenth and twentieth centuries: Europeanization and modernization. Although both trends began before the eighteenth and continued into the twentieth century, it was during those two hundred years that one may most clearly study the dynamics involved and draw from them comparative insights.

By modernization we mean a complex of changes in the intellectual, economic, social, and political spheres, each of which depended upon the other. The specific nature of these changes will become clear in the course of subsequent discussion, but some broad characteristics may be indicated here. First, man's view of himself and his place in the world was greatly modified. By the twentieth century a Latin American was more likely to see himself as potentially controlling nature through science than before. Second, society was no longer perceived as a divinely ordained and permanently ordered whole, imbued with a mystic quality that made it greater than the sum of its individual parts. Political institutions, therefore, were more freely (perhaps too freely) tinkered with. Third, the individual's place within society was no longer believed to be immutably fixed. The possibility of individual motion was greatly increased.

3

Fourth, economic activity was no longer controlled by monopolies, special concessions, general prohibitions, individual privileges, chartered companies, and closed craft guilds. The economy was more open to the free enterprise of any individual, and trade was no longer channeled and restricted through certain ports and to certain countries. Although by the twentieth century the technological innovations that characterize a modern economy had not—and may never—become typical of Latin America, the groundwork for any subsequent development was laid by these earlier changes.

The emancipation of Latin America from Spanish and Portuguese control accelerated this movement toward modernization. The new governments established direct commercial contacts with the capitalistic centers of Europe. The wars dislocated the old social relationships, and the corporate society was then taken apart piece by piece. Breaking the ties with the mother countries required the construction of alternative political models, a process deeply suggestive of the new relationship between man and his institutions. Although the process was never completed, the events from 1808 to 1825 contributed powerfully toward the modernization of Latin America.

By Europeanization we simply mean closer contacts with the mainstream of European development regardless of their particular results in America. More often than not, however, Europeanization led to modernization, for modernizing forces were disseminated from Europe. Not surprisingly, the strongest impetus toward modernization came from northern Europe because France and England were rising to preeminence while Spain was declining during the seventeenth and eighteenth centuries. The demands and requirements of the industrial revolution drove men, especially Englishmen, to search for new markets and new sources of raw materials, an activity that typified both the eighteenth and nineteenth centuries. Latin American cities became beachheads of European culture. The scientists who first awakened the interest of Latin Americans in the flora and fauna around them were usually from northern Europe, and the writers who first provided the Latin American intellectuals with new ideas regarding the organization of society were also from northern Europe. Instead of books by medieval Spanish mystics, the favorite authors—either read directly or understood through popularizations produced by Spanish writers—were Voltaire and Locke, Montesquieu and Adam Smith, Henri Say and Bentham, Comte and Spencer. One cannot, of course, think of this process only in terms of Anglo-Saxonization or northern-Europeanization because, aside from the awkwardness of the terms, much of the impulse for the initiation of change came from Spain. In all, between the eighteenth and twentieth centuries Latin America became more closely identified with the dynamic centers of European life; in this sense it became Europeanized.

The establishment of political independence was a major step toward Europeanization. Ironically the breaking of political ties with the mother countries moved Latin America toward integration with Europe. After independence more Latin Americans were apt to be driven by the same impulses and react to the same stimuli as Europeans and even to be more directly affected by decisions made in Europe.

So these terms, Europeanization and modernization, are used to indicate that Latin America underwent a major transformation after 1700 and that it was pulled in this direction by the widening currents of northern European influence, currents which sprang from the transformation of Europe itself.

Yet if we speak of Europeanization and modernization as major trends affecting all of Latin America we must not forget the divergent reactions of various regions and groups to these great forces. It would be poor history, as it is poor foreign policy, to ignore the variety of Latin America or to place all interest groups there in the same conceptual box; for some regions blossomed under the influence of European winds while others withered, and some groups and individuals rose while others declined. In order to compare local reactions to these broad trends we shall focus on the establishment of political independence in Latin America between 1808 and 1825. By grappling with these events, the student may not only come to judge the importance of the broader forces, but also become alert to the importance of the comparative approach in highlighting the complexities of the historical process.

But first we must look at the eighteenth century, for it was then that the processes of modernization and Europeanization really began. Indeed, although gradual and at times almost imperceptible, the transformations of that period were largely responsible for the support which the independence movements were later to secure.

POLITICAL
STRUCTURE

The eighteenth century began with the War of the Spanish Succession (1700–1713). Louis XIV of France decided to enforce his family's claim upon the throne of Spain and hoped eventually to unite the two kingdoms. In the end France and Spain remained forever separate, but a major branch of the Bourbon line did replace the Hapsburg dynasty on the throne of Spain. The first three Bourbon kings, Philip V (reigned 1700–1746), Ferdinand VI (1746–1759), and Charles III (1759–1788), inspired by the example of their French cousins and at first surrounded by French advisers, set to work to transform Spain; in so doing they wrought major changes upon Spanish America as well.

Perhaps the most important alterations made by the Bourbons were the result of their view of the relationship between king and subject, which sharply differed from that of the Hapsburgs. The Hapsburgs thought of themselves as patriarchs who occupied their position, not because of the divine right of kings, but because of the divine right of fathers. According to the Hapsburg view, God had ordained the family as the basic unit of society, and the family was hierarchically structured with the father at its head; therefore the king was also the head of a similarly structured family with every member of society occupying a place within it that was fixed by God. In a sense, the Hapsburgs ruled over a family, not a state. The basic political philosophy, which permeated the entire social organism, elicited and depended upon relationships of authority-dependency, benevolence-loyalty. No legislation could change the deeply meaningful link between king and subject, just as no law could alter the biological connection between father and son. The Bourbons thought somewhat differently about the relationship between king and subject. Although not entirely free of such a familial viewpoint, the Bourbons were more apt to think of the king as a ruler than as a father and to judge him by the efficiency of his rule rather than by his love for his subjects. The Spanish-Americans clung to the Hapsburg image of the patriarchal state and resisted the Bourbons' political philosophy.

Furthermore, the Spanish-Americans thought of themselves as united to Spain merely by their king. At the time of the discovery of America, Spain had been divided into distinct kingdoms united only by a common throne, and each kingdom had maintained its own traditional institutions, courts, and councils to advise the king on local affairs. The overseas empire became yet another kingdom with a separate council, known as the Council of the Indies, to advise the king on American affairs. The Council of the Indies was the highest administrative, legislative, and judicial body that the Spanish-Americans dealt with before appealing to the king. So, Spanish-Americans did not consider themselves colonials of Spain. When superimposed upon the patriarchal view of the state, this self-image became more than a legalistic distinction. These kingdoms were like distinct families with the same father; and if the father were to be removed, nothing would make one family subordinate to the other. In contrast, the Bourbons conceived of all Spanish territory as a single kingdom and believed that the purpose of the Spanish-American colonies was to advance the interests of Spain.

The Bourbons put a high value upon efficiency. In theory, at least, scientific administration was the keystone of their approach. Direct lines of command, the ability to pinpoint responsibility, clear separation of jurisdictions, and specialized functions were the goals of the reforms which the Bourbons imposed upon Spain and Spanish America. The Bourbons' first step toward change was to create a cabinet which met to consider the affairs of the entire realm whether in Aragon or in Spanish America. Then, impelled by the same logic, they broke up the affairs of the empire into component parts: for instance, military affairs were handled by the Minister of War, judicial matters by the Minister of Justice, and relations with other colonial powers by the

Minister of Foreign Affairs. The Council of the Indies dwindled in importance.

The inhabitants of Spain had long forgotten that Spanish America was a separate kingdom, for even under the Hapsburgs, Spaniards had usually been chosen to occupy the major posts in America: for instance, the viceroys, who represented the king in America, had almost invariably been Spaniards. The viceroys were advised by *audiencias,* a kind of miniature Council of the Indies that also acted as a court. Since its members dealt with the most vital questions and exercised great power, only the most learned and most trusted subjects of the king were appointed to *audiencias;* the appointees tended to be almost exclusively Spanish-born before the eighteenth century. So Spaniards came to think of the overseas kingdom as their American colonies.

The Bourbon kings believed that American affairs had to foster the welfare of Spain. As the eighteenth century wore on, they were increasingly aware that the economic life of Spanish America had to be revitalized if sufficient resources were to be marshaled to conduct Spain's frequent wars. Indeed, according to the Family Compact drawn up between the king of Spain and his cousin, the king of France, they determined that their common interests depended upon changes in the American administration. One such change was the application in Spanish America of the European system of intendants. Intendants were administrative representatives who reported only to the king and who had as their principal objective the increase of royal revenue by stimulating the local economy and enforcing the collection of taxes. In theory at least, the system of intendants was a perfect example of the Bourbons' belief in efficient, centralized administration. The application of this system meant the end of a complicated and extremely subdivided political system in which the viceroy had exerted his power through a large number of provincial officials of different ranks and titles. The old system was now replaced by a simplified structure of authority in which a relatively few intendants reported directly to the viceroy on some matters and directly to the king on matters of finance.

The Bourbons actually took vast areas completely out of the control of the two viceroys who had until then ruled all

Spanish America from their seats in Mexico City and Lima. In South America a whole series of new jurisdictions were created. In 1717, the Bourbons set up the Viceroyalty of New Granada (see map), encompassing the territory now included in Venezuela, Colombia, and Ecuador,* with its seat in Bogotá. In 1776, the Bourbons established the Viceroyalty of Río de la Plata (see map), stripping from the Viceroyalty of Peru most of the territory now included in Bolivia, Argentina, Paraguay, and Uruguay. Then they created two captaincies-general (virtually viceroyalties, but without as much prestige) for what are now Chile and Venezuela.

The Bourbons realized that they had to pay closer attention to the Viceroyalty of New Spain, the territory that is now Mexico and Central America. Its northern frontier was threatened by Russians, French, British, and marauding Indian tribes that were squeezed southward. But it was patently ridiculous to think of setting up a viceroyalty with all its accompanying pomp and ceremony in this sparsely settled region where the largest town was little more than a heap of adobes. So in 1776 the area that is today the northern states of Mexico and the southwestern United States was taken out of the jurisdiction of the viceroy in Mexico City and placed under a commandant general.

HACIENDA AND PLANTATION   The dominant feature of the land-tenure pattern in Spanish America by the eighteenth century was the hacienda, or large landed estate. A basic value among the upper classes, probably inculcated in childhood, was that land was the only legitimate symbol of status. The origins of this attitude lay deep in the Spanish past, and it was bolstered by legal devices such as the entailed estate, which made it impossible to divide up some properties at the death of the owner. When the conquistadors arrived in the highlands, they found millions of Indians accustomed to a master-man relationship, prepared to labor on land that was not individually theirs, and able to carry on agricultural activity without much supervision; thus it was only natural that the

---

* For the sake of simplicity all areas are henceforth referred to by their modern names.

first Spaniards should adopt the large estate. Subsequently the bulk of the tillable land was so divided.

The hacienda became a basic Spanish-American economic and social unit—really more social than economic in significance, for the hacienda was held primarily for its status-contributing value and not for profit. The produce of the hacienda went to feed the workers, to supply the owner's town-house kitchen, and to be exchanged in barter for the luxuries required for urban living. Otherwise the owner was not concerned with its productivity. The workers were paid in the limited right to use small plots of land for themselves and in goods at the company store. Because these goods were advanced at prices that could not possibly be met by the workers, a system of debt-slavery resulted. The system was perpetual since both custom and law made it impossible to seek other employment until the debt had been repaid. The result was the peon, or debt-slave. He grew up on the hacienda, inherited his father's debt, and passed it on, considerably augmented, to his son.

Yet, hard as it is for us to imagine, the system was characterized by a great deal of mutuality and consent. The paternalism of the Hapsburg kings was matched by that of the *hacendado,* or owner, who thought of his peons as his children. He saw that the peons were treated when they were sick, got them out of jail after a drunken Saturday-night brawl, and provided an occasional visit by a priest to take care of their spiritual needs. He would have been shocked had he been called an exploiter. The peons, in turn, were loyal and loving. On the owner's birthday, the peons would shower him with gifts. It was a family, and its familial character was reinforced by the system of *compadrazgo:* the owner became the godfather of the peon's children and thus assumed, through ritual, the position of close relative. In this and in other ways the owner became the surrogate of the king and even of God. Unfortunately for his "children," like God and king the owner did not often choose to live on the hacienda. He much preferred town life and left the administration of his estate in the hands of the mayordomo whose sense of responsibility was only to the *hacendado* and never to the peon.

The hacienda was only very indirectly touched by the

international economy. The primary export from Spanish America was bullion, and European demands were linked to the agricultural activity on the hacienda only by the demand for foodstuffs to feed the workers in the mines or the inhabitants of the cities whose sophisticated culture the mines financed.

During the eighteenth century a new institution became prominent: the plantation. Changing economic needs in Europe account for its rise. More leisure and the affluence of the European urban class created a market for tropical luxuries, such as sugar and tobacco. Products, such as cotton, cattle hides, and tallow, were needed to supply the expanding European industries. Added to these new demands was the local stimulus to search for new products as a financial substitute for silver and gold, which had declined through the failure to adopt new techniques to deal with ores of low quality.

These new stimuli were significant. Plantations were operated for profit and not owned merely for status. They were not devoted to subsistence agriculture or to supplying the relatively inelastic demand of local towns; they were plugged into the expanding and dynamic European economy. In contrast to the many haciendas that still survived, the plantations were often owned by new arrivals from Spain who knew of the demand, had contacts with international merchants, and possessed the enterprise and drive to establish new ventures.

The ancient ties of man to land were broken by the plantation. The center of Indian population had been the highland areas, but tropical exports were produced in sparsely populated lowland regions. Either the Indians would have to be moved into an environment to which they were unaccustomed or slaves would have to be imported from Africa. Iberian peoples had been accustomed to African slave labor for centuries; they had used African slaves on the Atlantic islands (for example, Madeira and the Canaries) before the discovery of America and had introduced them into the New World in the sixteenth century. With the expanding needs of invigorated plantation economies, it was only natural that plantation owners looked with heightened interest for labor in Africa. Slave traders, especially the

British, brought in an ever-increasing number of human cargoes. The Bourbons even issued a new slave code to stimulate the use of black slaves by abolishing the ancient slave-trade monopolies. Whether slaves or free Indians lured down from the mountains by cash wages, these workers on the plantations lacked a sense of loyalty toward their master; and he regarded them only as factors of production, the cost of which must be carefully balanced out against profits.

The new economic activities also implied a shift in the center of economic gravity away from the mining areas and toward new centers, previously on the frontiers. This fact is especially noticeable in Spanish South America: Lima in the west began to lose ground while Caracas in the north and Buenos Aires in the south increased in importance. Mexico City managed to cash in on both the old and the new economic activity, but even in Mexico the coastal regions entered a period of new importance.

TRADE   Before the eighteenth century, all Spanish-controlled trans-Atlantic trade centered on four ports: Cádiz in Spain and Cartagena, Panamá, and Veracruz in America. The inflexible mentality of the Hapsburgs and the practical necessity of protecting the silver-laden ships that sailed from America against hostile and semiofficial pirates determined the use of fleets protected by men-of-war. The ships that came from Spain, therefore, were required to leave the port of Cádiz together and were not allowed to separate until they were safely in the Caribbean Sea. The result was, for example, that manufactured goods produced in England to be consumed in Argentina went first to Spain and then to Panamá, next by sea to Lima along the relatively safe Pacific coast, and then overland across the towering mountains and broad plains to Argentina. In Spain only Cádiz was permitted to participate, for the merchant guild held great political power and was the first on the commercial scene. And in each of the entrepôts through which goods passed, other merchants, often the agents for the Cádiz monopolists, had maintained a tight hold on the profitable interchange.

If Spain had produced the goods, it might have been able to maintain this commercial system indefinitely, but this was not the case; smuggling became the bane of royal administrators in the Americas. Sometimes through war and sometimes through subterfuge, the English managed to invade the American markets, exchanging cottons and knives for cacao, sugar, and hides. During the first part of the eighteenth century smuggling increased rapidly. Non-Spanish masters had the daring, the Spanish-Americans, especially those outside the monopoly ports, had the desire for cheaper goods, and Spanish officials often connived to make this a widespread practice.

Eventually, the Bourbons set to work to reform and modernize the commercial system. First, they liberalized the regulations, making it easier and cheaper to trade legally through Spain. Second, they created monopoly companies modeled on the Dutch or British East India Companies in which capitalists from other parts of Spain besides Cádiz could participate. These companies were assigned special areas in the Americas as their preserve to defend and develop. Finally, a steadily increasing number of ports were opened and allowed to trade with each other. The fleet system was ultimately abandoned. The culmination of this policy was the so-called Decree of Free Trade (1778), which allowed twenty-four ports in America to trade with almost any port in Spain. Commerce was still limited to Spanish subjects, and in effect, still fell into the hands of the great Spanish merchants who had the necessary capital; but the decree was a great boon to ports like Buenos Aires that had previously suffered most from the restrictions.

HIERARCHY, POWER, AND EDUCATION   The Hapsburg political and economic structure had been reinforced by an inherited social hierarchy in which everyone had a fixed position within society. Every man was born to a place, and his condition was immutable and that of his children was the same as his. Each corporation—guild, religious order, or military rank—had its special rights and privileges. The guild system is an example. The goldsmiths and the shoemakers were each organized as a family in which the journeymen, as virtual children, were in a fixed relationship to the masters. Each guild had its particular identifying clothes, its own patron saint, its own section of town, and its own court where masters passed judgment over cases involving conflicts between themselves and journeymen or between themselves and members of less privileged corporations. Similarly, in Spanish America the stockmen had their own guild and court where large landowners judged the fate of alleged cattle rustlers; and the merchants had their own guild dominated by wealthy merchants who engaged in international trade. The right to special clothes, special courts, special places in parades, and other honors were called, collectively, *fueros*. The judicial system, thus divided up by occupation and corporation, reflected the Hapsburg view of society. Instead of being formed by individuals protected in their rights and mobile in relationship to one another, society was made up of castes, classes, and corporations, layered one atop another or lying side by side.

The position of the Bourbon kings with regard to the social hierarchy was somewhat ambiguous. In some ways the Bourbons worked to destroy it, but in other ways they bolstered it or at least came to terms with it; for instance, in their effort to revitalize the mining industry, the Bourbons created a guild for mine-owners with special rights and privileges in order to encourage an occupation considered less prestigious than landowning. The mining guild was naturally granted its own court to adjudicate questions arising within mining legislation and this seemed to fit the older corporate structure of society. But the guild also supervised the new school of mines in Mexico in which the latest scientific principles were taught and a rational attitude toward the world was inculcated. Social mobility was its natural concomitant.

Although the corporate structure of society remained relatively unchanged, class divisions may have intensified. The lot of the Indians, for instance, became worse on the plantation. Their position, as had been true for the common Indians even in the days of their great pre-Columbian civilizations, was that of a servile and obedient peasantry. Although the Indian nobility had been cleverly alienated from their fellows and had even intermarried with the conquistadors, the bulk of the Indians lived in subhuman conditions, as most of them still do today.

At the other extreme of the social spectrum were the creoles, persons of Spanish descent born in America. The creoles occupied many rungs of society but, along with some Spaniards, monopolized the most prestigious social positions, shutting out the Indians and mestizos. The great landowners formed a creole aristocracy that was acutely class-conscious and liked to lord it over other groups, but they were looked down upon by the Spaniards born in Spain. One of the instruments of the Spanish-born was the myth of creole inferiority, that is, the belief that the American climate, or perhaps the American longitude, was somehow enervating. By nature, people born and raised in America, regardless of their parentage, were thought to lack intelligence, drive, and stamina. This idea is no more ridiculous than many of the prejudices that are still found among us today and was even accepted by many of the creoles.

Perhaps the saving grace of the Spanish colonial system was that the creoles did not monopolize all political power. They could amass great fortunes, operate huge estates, and hold all other American groups in contempt, but they could not run the government entirely in their own behalf, for the Spanish occupied the chief positions of power and tended to scorn the pretensions of the creoles. Spanish bureaucrats were more responsive to the wishes of the king and often tried to ameliorate the condition of the Indians over the opposition of the creoles.

The creoles could still exercise a vestige of governmental responsibility in the *cabildo*. These councils had been charged with county and city government, but they had gradually lost whatever power they had because an increasing number of petty details were covered by laws issued from Madrid. Furthermore, as the crown became more desperate for money, it had often sold, sometimes in perpetuity, the seats on the *cabildo;* therefore, few people looked to the *cabildo* as a source of vitality or new ideas. The intendants sent out by the Bourbon kings in the eighteenth century often gave them new life by their reforms, but, in general, the *cabildos* in the principal cities remained the refuge of mediocrity, filled by descendants of once-eminent families. The exceptions to this rule were to be found in the more remote locations, the frontier towns where new problems were frequent and royal control was weak.

Evidence of creole inferiority, said the Spaniards, was

their propensity for "refined" and purposeless education. Spanish America had several universities. In the sixteenth century the universities in Mexico and Lima had ranked with the best in Spain. But none of the Spanish-American universities had spent much effort on self-renovation. Cut off from Europe not only by the Atlantic but also by the declining vitality of Spain itself, the universities had become scenes of decadence by the end of the seventeenth century. Most higher education was designed to satisfy the needs of the creole aristocracy by giving them the ability to drop Latin phrases at the appropriate moment, to compose poetry, to recite correctly from memory certain legal and theological formulae, and to make a living without dirtying their hands. The result was a class of graduates alienated from the problems of their land.

During the eighteenth century, however, this situation was changed significantly by the European Enlightenment. This is not the place to discuss the nature of this complex intellectual movement in either America or Europe nor to elaborate the point that the Spanish-Americans picked and chose from this intellectual smorgasbord according to their special needs, but it must be noted here that the view of man and of the world which the Enlightenment embodied was diametrically opposed to the one which had been most prevalent in Spanish America under the Hapsburgs.

Enlightenment thought exerted a considerable impact on Latin America. It is no longer necessary to attack the myth that Spanish America was kept in cloistered isolation from all new ideas by a veritable iron curtain imposed by the retrograde Spanish government. The truth is that precisely this government, led by "enlightened despots," did what it could to inject a modern world view into backward overseas domains. But, as many a Peace Corps Volunteer has since found out, it is not easy to transform the basic attitudes, values, and point of view of traditional societies; and the spread of the Enlightenment must not be exaggerated in a society within which only the narrowest fringe could even read and write.

Surprising as it may seem, science—and all that it implies regarding man's place in the world—was the most important aspect of the new thought in Latin America. The avenues for communicating its new approach were not restricted. Scientific expeditions working under official auspices were perhaps the most important. Some noted European astronomers, botanists, and geographers were sent out at royal expense to conduct studies, collect specimens, observe the stars, and make meticulous drawings. Some of the most conservative centers were abandoning or manipulating the scholasticism inherited from medieval days. Even in the relatively isolated university of Guatemala the "new thought" was fully accepted by professors and dutifully repeated in student theses.

A fascinating example of the new scientific spirit in America was José Celestino Mutis (1732–1808), a Spanish physician who had moved to Bogotá in the early 1760s. As trained personnel was scarce, he was asked to teach mathematics and astronomy at the university where he subsequently built an observatory and taught the Copernican system. With characteristic eighteenth-century curiosity, Mutis then began the study of botany and carried on an active correspondence with Carolus Linnaeus. The viceroy, with the encouragement of the Spanish government, provided him with a subsidy to begin a vast botanical project to make a systematic collection of specimens and drawings of South American flora. His botanical work was carried on by his pupil Francisco José de Caldas (1770–1816), who kept up an active correspondence and intellectual interchange with Benjamin Franklin, perhaps the most important Enlightenment thinker in the New World. Eventually Caldas turned his attention to institutional obstacles to change.

The social and political ideas associated with the Enlightenment also invaded Spanish America although without the same official protection. In Spain the new ideas had been popularized by Benito Feijóo and, although many of the original sources were banned by the *Index* of prohibited books, other writers spread their concepts far and near. Anyway there were many aristocratic creoles who directly knew the works of Voltaire, Rousseau, and Montesquieu, and attempts to suppress the circulation of their views were always in vain. On the other hand, the spread of these ideas in Spanish America was dependent upon the acceptance of the new world view based on science. It was only at the time of independence itself that the social and political implications of the new ideology became really important among the creoles.

Between the creoles and the Indians were the mestizos, persons of mixed white and Indian parentage. It is sometimes estimated that only 600,000 Spaniards ever migrated to America; but, through race mixture more than through force, they imposed their culture over a vast empire. Despite this contribution, the mestizos occupied a distinctly inferior social position, accepted by neither the Indians nor the whites. The mestizos were restless, ambitious, and anxious to prove that they were just as good as the whites. As a consequence the mestizos were aggressive and often resentful, for, despite their efforts, they did not frequently succeed. For this reason and because of their irregular upbringing, the mestizos were often the delinquents of society.

These distinctions among classes seem to have been more economic than racial. Although most mestizos remained lowly, there were numerous examples of mestizos who, becoming wealthy, were able to buy their way into the white world for themselves or their descendants and be accepted in society as whites. On the other hand, the mestizos' ability to compete with the creoles intensified prejudice. Creoles resented the fact that the Spaniards, especially the bureaucrats sent out by the Bourbon kings, seemed to be more concerned with place of birth than with race. During the eighteenth century it may well be that racist feeling was on the increase in Spanish America.

RELIGION  Under the Hapsburgs, State and Church had been so closely related that they should be considered one; a conceptual distinction between them may be misleading unless it is understood as merely an heuristic device. For centuries the king had been granted patronage over the Church; that is, the crown would finance and foster the preaching of the gospel and, in return, would make all appointments. In addition, the crown would collect the tithe, a tax for Church purposes, and dispense it according to its own lights. Even papal bulls could be published only after they had been approved by State officials, who also controlled the introduction of religious orders and the travels of individual friars. Finally, the Inquisition was primarily an arm of the State designed to maintain ideological purity. That one individual might simultaneously be viceroy and archbishop is a good example of the fusion of Church and State.

It was fortunate that the State controlled the Church, for its enormous wealth, especially if one includes that of the religious orders, might otherwise have represented an unregulated and irresponsible power. The ordinary expenses of the bishops, cathedrals, and parish priests were paid by the State from the revenue derived from the tithe. But, in addition, the Church received numerous bequests. To die without giving substantial property to the Church was to reveal a great lack of foresight. After the land was given to the Church, it was rarely sold, either because it was inalienable by the terms of the bequest or because the Church, unlike individuals, was never forced to divide its property among its heirs. Furthermore, since the laws of usury were enforced with medieval strictures, the only banker in Spanish America was the Church. As many landowners lived beyond their means, it held foreclosable mortgages on a vast number of estates.

Much of this wealth was used to finance charitable institutions and mission work. The social services which are today thought of as the government's responsibility were then carried on by the Church which, to repeat, was no more than a branch of the State. Hospitals, alms houses, schools, and colleges were maintained at Church expense. Although many of these institutions fell into disrepair and became merely sinecures for churchmen primarily interested in luxurious living in the cities, others continued to be vigorous centers of social concern. In addition, the imperial task of extending the frontiers of Spanish culture and Spanish power into the jungles of South and Central America and into the treeless plains of North America was carried out by courageous missionaries.

The Bourbon kings maintained the union of Church and State but were much more conscious of the Church as a separate entity. Probably for this reason, there was more friction between the crown and the Church during the eighteenth century. The best example of mutual distrust was the case of the Jesuits. The Bourbons, aware of the fact that this religious order was more loyal to the pope than to the king, deeply resented its strength and vitality. Furthermore, the Jesuits in America were among the most efficient administrators of property, owned some of the best land, competed successfully with the local merchants, operated the leading secondary schools, and, through their vigor and their drive, created intense jealousies wherever they went. Finally Charles III ordered their expulsion from all Spanish territory. The act was carried out simultaneously throughout the empire in 1767 and preparations for it were kept as secret as could be done; but it nevertheless resulted in uprisings among some Indians and lower-class groups over whom the Jesuits had maintained a protective stance.

PORTUGUESE AMERICA  Conditions in Brazil were markedly different from those in the highlands of Spanish America. The Indians living in Brazil at the time of first contact with Europeans had not been highly civilized Aztecs or Incas but rather were naked savages who roamed the wilds with bows and arrows in search of game, infrequently planting and harvesting some corn and manioc. For this reason, the Indians had not located sources of gold and precious stones. The Portuguese, despite diligent searching, were not to find these coveted supplies until the end of the seventeenth century. By that time the basic institutional structure of Brazil was set. Sugar had become the chief export crop and the principal activity of the settlers.

Instead of Indian laborers, the land was principally worked by African slaves. The sugar plantation gave Brazil a rural cast; for instance, the isolated chapel occupied by a plantation chaplain was the center of religious life rather than the city cathedral. Perhaps because African slaves had been extensively used in Brazil for much longer or because in the eighteenth century the sugar economy was in decline, master-slave relationships on the Brazilian plantations tended to be more similar to those between *hacendado* and peon on the Spanish-American hacienda than to those of masters and slaves on the corresponding plantation. Hundreds of thousands of enslaved blacks had been imported to Brazil, and the Portuguese mixed with them carelessly; the Brazilian planters were not as apt to scorn the resulting mulatto as were the Spanish. Meanwhile, the Indian was rapidly eliminated from the coastal region and pushed back into the interior.

From the beginning, Brazil had received less attention from Lisbon than Spanish America from Madrid. The real empire of Portugal in the early sixteenth century had been India and the spice islands. Brazil, without precious minerals, had been only a second thought, and the Portuguese paid scant attention to it unless it was threatened by other nations. Thus the Portuguese Americans were practically left to govern themselves. The basic unit of government, beyond the plantation itself, was the *câmara*, a municipal or county council. The *câmara* was dominated by planters who, in contrast to their Spanish counterparts in the *cabildo*, could wield real power through it either because the *câmaras* were too far from Portugal to be effectively controlled or because they had been granted rights, privileges, and exemptions by careless Portuguese kings.

The Portuguese had never centralized trade in Lisbon, so it was really impossible to maintain an efficient fleet system. When Portugal was ruled by Spanish kings between 1580 and 1640, the Hapsburgs despaired in their efforts to impose an orderly commercial system upon it. Trade could be carried on directly with Portugal from every Brazilian port, and even foreign ships were occasionally given legal permission to trade there.

Finally, the Portuguese differed from the Spanish in cultural traits that are hard to define. The Spanish were more likely to hold unyielding prejudices and be committed to absolute ideals; the Portuguese were less rigid and did not seem to take themselves so seriously. Religious orthodoxy was always less important to the Portuguese, and the Spaniards looked upon them as degenerate worshippers of Baal. Both the Spanish and Portuguese expelled Jews from their countries, but the Portuguese were less adamant in their persecution. For the Spanish one precondition for migrating to Spanish America was the purity of one's "blood," that is, religion; but the Portuguese encouraged the "New Christians," that is, converts from Judaism and their descendants, to migrate to Brazil.

In one way the Brazilian experience was similar to that of Spanish America: the eighteenth century was full of change. Curiously, by changing in opposite directions they became more similar. Brazil became more interested in mines just as Spanish America was turning toward plantations. The mines discovered in the province of Minas Gerais finally gave Brazil the wealth and importance it had previously lacked. Cities now flourished, and Brazilians had the leisure to engage in the arts for the first time. At last a viceroy was appointed to oversee the various provincial governors.

The wealth that poured in from Brazil also enabled Portugal to carry on a reinvigorated government. The "enlightened despot" of Portugal was not a king but the Marquis of Pombal, who, as chief minister, obtained such an ascendancy over the king that he was virtually dictator from 1750 to 1777. He took a decidedly developmental attitude toward the Portuguese economy, fostering agriculture and encouraging industry. He successfully took up an old plan to lessen the deleterious effect of the Inquisition upon "New Christian" businessmen. He reorganized the public services, ended all slavery in Portugal, and abolished Indian slavery in Brazil. He could be frightfully cruel and made many political prisoners, but he also won a great deal of respect for his reforming zeal and great energy, especially in rebuilding the city of Lisbon devastated by the earthquake of 1755. Like Charles III he was deeply suspicious of the Jesuits, whom he charged with plotting with the Spanish to prevent the extension of Portuguese boundaries in South America in areas where the Jesuits maintained missions. Portugal was one of the first nations in Europe to order the expulsion of the Jesuits.

*　　*　　*

The major thrust of eighteenth-century change in Spanish and Portuguese America was toward its reincorporation into the mainstream of Western civilization. By 1700 Spain and Portugal had themselves become isolated from the dynamic centers of European life; the Bourbon kings and the Marquis of Pombal broke down that isolation. Attempts at increased efficiency in government reflected the innovative and scientific approach to institutional life typical of modern man. Plantation agriculture in Spanish America was the result of closer economic contacts with Europe and resulted in a more modern, albeit cruel, social relationship between man and master. By the same token, mining wealth in Brazil prompted the growth of a more mobile and impersonal social structure. A new view of society meant a new view of its religious underpinnings, and both Spanish and Portuguese rulers now tended intellectually to separate Church and State, even going so far as to expel an entire religious order from their dominions. True, the corporate social structure remained one whole, although the eighteenth century intensified the tension among creoles, mestizos, and Indians. The overall impression left by an examination of this period is that Latin America now began to feel the strengthening though still gentle pull of a modernizing, capitalistic, urban, secular, and individualistic spirit.

# Chapter 2

# Reactions
# to Change

The impact of Europeanization and modernization differed from place to place and from group to group. Reactions to the independence movements, an expression of these larger forces, were consequently to vary too. This chapter will examine the bases of these differences in Argentina and Chile.

ARGENTINA:   The Viceroyalty of Río de la Plata lacked geographical and
REGIONS   historical unity and was unwieldly as a government unit from the time of its establishment in 1776. The viceroyalty contained a variety of regions: the massive Andean ranges then referred to as Alto Peru and since renamed Bolivia; the piedmont regions that are now in Argentina, which included the wine-producing zone around Mendoza, the sugar-rich areas around Tucumán, and the proud and ancient university of Córdoba; and the steaming lowlands that are today Paraguay. At the center of the viceroyalty lay the vast pampas, or grassy plains, that stretched for nearly 500 miles west of the city of Buenos Aires. Cattle roamed free and wild on the pampas, multiplying rapidly during two hundred years of neglect. Almost as wild as the cattle were the gauchos, or plainsmen, who slaughtered the cattle for their hides. And finally, the viceroyalty included the grasslands that are today Uruguay.

The defense of this last region against incursions from

the Portuguese was the chief reason for the introduction of viceregal pomp and ceremony into the otherwise bedraggled country village of Buenos Aires. The Portuguese had established a settlement directly across the estuary of the Río de la Plata in 1680, and from this base they had carried on successful smuggling activity. Whenever war broke out in eighteenth-century Europe, Spain and Portugal were on opposite sides of the struggle, and repercussions were immediate in this region. During the fighting the Spaniards usually drove the Portuguese out of the region along the eastern bank of the Río de la Plata estuary and pushed them into what is today southern Brazil, but at the ensuing peace conference the Portuguese would regain much of the lost territory and then surreptitiously extend their control still farther into this sparsely settled region. Finally in 1776 King Charles III dispatched to the region ten thousand troops and a viceroy charged with putting a stop to Portuguese expansion. Although the king was momentarily successful in this goal, the region remained a pawn fought over by Portuguese- and Spanish-speaking peoples even after the viceroyalty was succeeded by independent republics.

A great rivalry existed between the two cities in the region: Buenos Aires and Montevideo. The harbor was better at Montevideo than at Buenos Aires, and the surrounding region was considered far richer in pastoral resources than the pampas around Buenos Aires; yet Buenos Aires was favored by the Bourbons. The appointment of a viceroy to Buenos Aires exacerbated these tensions, and deep and ingrained hostility between the two cities was the final result.

The Decree of Free Trade of 1778 had even more far-reaching results. Buenos Aires was permitted to trade directly with Spain instead of indirectly via Lima and the circuitous route that led along the Pacific coast through Panamá and across the Caribbean and Atlantic to Spain. The transformations were profound. No longer strangled by isolation from international markets and foreign sources of supply, no longer forced to survive only by virtue of its smugglers' ability, the region around Buenos Aires experienced rapid economic growth. Prices of imports declined, and a large legal export business developed. The major export products were hides, horns, jerked beef, and tallow, which came from the cattle that roamed the pampas. Buenos Aires, whose inhabitants were called *porteños,* became the port for a vast and wealthy area, exporting not only to Spain, but also to the Caribbean. The population of the city grew from twelve thousand in 1750 to fifty thousand by 1800.

Satisfaction with the trade reform was short-lived. By the end of the century, most of the cattle had been slaughtered, and the years of unrestrained prosperity had only served to whet the appetite for an easier exchange of products between Buenos Aires and other European nations, particularly England. Furthermore Spain lagged behind England in her ability to supply manufactured goods and continued to burden the exchange of goods with onerous taxes designed to bolster her own faltering finances. England was the largest consumer of exports and the chief supplier of imports. Spain merely stood in the way of continued economic expansion by preventing a better balance in the prices of exports and imports.

Yet Spain could not open the port of Buenos Aires to the trade of European nations because this would have destroyed her monopoly merchants, whose political power was considerable, and would have been unjust to the traditionally loyal western cities, particularly Lima. So, by the beginning of the nineteenth century, greater prosperity for the pampas became logically synonymous with independence from Spain, even when that conclusion was not actually expressed.

ARGENTINA: GROUPS

By 1810 there was a complete lack of consensus among the divergent groups as to the organization of society and its government. Subsequently the divisions became ever more intense, and new sources of friction were added to old ones. Four issues served as principal sources of disagreement. First, in ultimate importance, was the issue of social structure: Should the old corporate society, hierarchic in conception and religious in basis, be continued, or should it be replaced by a modern society of free individuals, vertically mobile regardless of original "condition"? Second, and most immediately in evidence before 1810, was the issue of trade:

Should trade be monopolized by Spain or opened to other nations? Third, and most apparent after 1810, was the issue of type of government: Should Argentina be ruled by a king—any king—or be a republic? And, finally, there remained what was to be the most enduring issue: the division deriving from divergent regional interests between federalists, who demanded provincial autonomy, and their opponents, who dreamed of a unified, centralized government. Although the issues are simply defined, they were not simply resolved, for individuals grouped and regrouped around each question without consistency. Even economic interests, social relationships, or educational levels did not ensure a common position on many of these issues.

The creole intellectuals were the most prominent early group to express opinions. Chiefly concentrated in Buenos Aires, but also existing in minute numbers in the interior cities, these men were inspired by the ideals of the Enlightenment, the French and American revolutions, and the desire to transform their country into a modern nation. Such men as Mariano Moreno (1778–1811), Manuel Belgrano (1770–1820), and Bernardino Rivadavia (1780–1845) were typical. The intellectuals believed that the natural laws that ruled over economic and social affairs required the end of commercial restrictions, the freedom of speech and press, and the attraction of immigrants from the non-Spanish world. They were divided, however, on the ideal form of government. Some wanted a monarchy on the British model; others, a republic. Some wanted a strong, centralized government that could impose modern change upon the backward interior; others, more doctrinaire, felt that freedom could only be preserved through local self-government and a loose federation of sovereign states. When independence became a reality, these divisions loomed larger in importance.

Merchants in Buenos Aires formed another group. This group was divided into the Spanish-born monopoly merchants, who preferred to maintain the old regime, and the moderately wealthy creole merchants, who envied the former's position. The latter shared the intellectuals' belief in the necessity for direct trade with northern Europe, but they were not as committed to the general transformation of the social structure as the intellectuals were. The more conservative merchants believed that a monarchy was the best form of government. All the merchants, however, wanted a centralized government, for they believed that this type of government would help place economic power in their hands and prevent internal tariff barriers from weakening their control over the country at large. After 1810 the merchants became more united.

The merchants in the interior cities differed sharply from their counterparts in Buenos Aires. They looked back nostalgically to the days of their own importance, were against the rupture of the old trading system, and opposed the centralization of government in Buenos Aires. They were naturally supported by craftsmen and agrarian interests of the interior.

The landowners and cattle ranchers in the huge province of Buenos Aires were anxious to establish direct commercial connections with the consuming centers of northern Europe and were, therefore, willing to go along with the suggestion of the intellectuals that the social structure must be transformed. They were upwardly mobile, lusting after wealth, and they had little use for the ancient modalities of social hierarchy, for the practices of entail and primogeniture, or for privilege and monopoly. After 1810 they gradually became more preoccupied with power and the protection of their interests. Not ideologically committed to central government, they managed outwardly to support federalists in the subsequent internecine fighting while instituting de facto strong centralized government whenever they occupied the seats of power. Thus there were many distinct groups and different regions in Argentina, and their reactions to the independence movement were not characterized by uniformity.

CHILE: REGIONS   Just as the creation of the Viceroyalty of Río de la Plata reduced the area under the jurisdiction of the viceroy in Lima, so too did the formation in 1778 of the Captaincy-General of Chile. Although this area along the west coast of South America was still nominally within the Viceroyalty of Peru, the king's agent, in effect, was the captain general who ruled from Santiago.

The Captaincy-General of Chile contained only one important region: the central valley, running for 600 miles north and south between the towering Andes on the east and the lower coastal range on the west. The land was chiefly used for the cultivation of wheat and other cereals, some viniculture, and the production of fruits, which were dried and exported. Cattle hides, pack mules, and small amounts of copper were also exported. All these goods went primarily to supply the market at Lima or the mines of Bolivia.

CHILE:
GROUPS

The central valley had been won from fierce Araucanian Indians two and a half centuries before, but in the heavily forested area south of the valley there still remained unconquered tribes, which included approximately 100,000 Indians. Those who had been conquered had been absorbed through racial mixture, and mestizos formed the bulk of the population. They were tenant farmers, farm hands, menial workers, domestic servants, and skilled artisans.

The creole landowners, on the whole, claimed descent from the original conquistadors and were anxious to hide their small admixture of Indian blood. In the eighteenth century this class was renovated by intermarriage with the sons and daughters of Basque immigrants, whose industry rapidly enabled them to accumulate considerable wealth. The landowners loved to entail their properties, purchase titles of nobility, and live in relative splendor in the cities with only occasional visits to their estates. However, they were frequently the victims of exploitation by Peruvian merchants who manipulated the price of wheat and the debtors of Peruvian counting houses that financed their opulent style of life. Furthermore, the carrying trade at the Chilean port of Valparaiso was also controlled by the Peruvians; by refusing to supply shipping at certain moments, they forced down the price of grain even in Chile. The landowners, therefore, were overjoyed by the Bourbons' trade reform, which allowed them to sell their grain all along the Pacific coast and to expand their exports across the Andes, or around Cape Horn, to Argentina. They did not seriously contemplate the possibility of exporting their goods to Europe.

The merchants of Santiago and its port, Valparaiso, were mostly Spanish-born, subagents of Lima houses, or agents of Spanish firms. Some creoles were merchants. They participated actively in contraband trade, but the influx of goods legally imported from Europe had by the 1800s already saturated the meager Chilean market and exhausted all available currency. Many merchants in legitimate and illegal trade went bankrupt. Moreover, the long struggle between merchants in Santiago and those in Lima culminated in the success of the former: the creole merchants were granted the right to establish their own *consulado,* and a mint was established in Santiago. Along with the Bourbon system of free trade, these measures helped to quell most of the complaints.

In Santiago, Valparaiso, and Concepción, a small group of intellectuals were active in the last years of the eighteenth century. Swept on especially by the reforms being carried out in Spain and the ideas being propagated there, but also by the ideas of Adam Smith and the French philosophes, these men were able to move in at crucial moments to influence the course of events. Since they could not make a particularly strong case for the right to export products directly to Europe, they found other issues: They played upon the dissatisfaction of both the merchants and landowners over taxes imposed by Spain, especially those collected at the end of the century to fight the English and, alternatively, the French, and the age-long resentment over the lack of political power. The intellectuals maintained that prosperity would only come when Chile was controlled by Chileans, by which, of course, they meant the small crust of creole aristocracy. The diversification of agriculture, the establishment of industries, and the introduction of modern techniques were all dependent, they said, upon a philosophy of government that had, as its chief aim, development rather than the immediate supply of revenues to the mother country. Once the revenues remained in Chile, progressive measures could be taken to facilitate rather than hinder the economy, and Chileans could take a stronger stand vis-à-vis the Peruvian merchants. Playing upon these ideas, the intellectuals managed to widen the circle of their listeners, but they would never have been able to do much if it were not for the constitutional crisis that overtook the Spanish empire at the time.

\* \* \*

If we compare Chile and Argentina, several points become clear. To begin with, one may note important similarities. The belief in modernization appealed to the intellectuals in the two regions, although they chose to emphasize different issues; and the desire to make decisions for themselves characterized both elites. Less similar, but still comparable, is the reaction of the landowners in the two regions. Although as heirs to ancient families the landowners of Chile were more conservative than the arriviste cattle ranchers of eastern Argentina; at least they were not threatened with ruin, as were the landowners of western Argentina, by the changing patterns of trade and the other social and economic modifications of the era. So the landowners responded more or less favorably to the promise of modernization.

Next, one is struck by three major differences. First, the possibility of direct exports of local products to northern Europe was of overriding importance in Argentina, but hardly considered in Chile. Second, the promise of cheaper imports was much more attractive to Argentina than to Chile. Third, Chile was more concerned with the preeminence of Lima, which was weakening under the Bourbons, than with throwing off the yoke of Spanish power. As was true for Uruguayans and Argentines, the rivalry between colonial centers often loomed larger than the conflict between creoles and Spaniards. Each of these three points contradicts a generalization that is often made about the origins of Latin American independence movements and thus demonstrates the advantage of a comparative approach.

Furthermore, one may distinguish three distinct responses to Europeanization and modernization. On the east coast, both Buenos Aires and Montevideo responded with enthusiasm. Closer contacts with the European industrial centers meant more profits. Although Montevideo differed from Buenos Aires in the way it responded, its opposition was not an expression of reluctance to engage in closer contacts with the expanding forces of international economy, but rather an objection to the supremacy of Buenos Aires. On the west coast, Chile hardly responded to Europeanization because the impulse of northern European trade was not yet felt, but she responded to modernization as much as Buenos Aires and Montevideo did. The interior cities of Argentina found their interests threatened by the very changes that Buenos Aires, Montevideo, and Chile welcomed: Europeanization and modernization spelt decline. These divergent responses deeply affected the course of the Latin American independence movements.

# Chapter 3

# Lords
# and Servants

All of Latin America was characterized by sharp class divisions, but in Venezuela and Mexico these divisions directly affected the course of the independence movements. In Venezuela the opposition of less favored groups stymied the wealthy creoles, and in Mexico an outburst of class hatred provoked a conservative reaction among otherwise progressive creoles. To understand the diverse course of these events, this chapter will analyze the situation in both countries at the beginning of the nineteenth century.

VENEZUELA: REGIONS The Viceroyalty of New Granada included at its eastern portion the area that is today Venezuela. Venezuela had been named a Captaincy-General a year earlier than Chile, and thus was practically removed from the jurisdiction of the viceroy of Bogotá.

Along its northern coast the hot, humid climate was ideal for the production of tobacco, indigo, and especially cacao. In the higher elevations of the piedmont immediately to the south of the coast coffee beans were grown. Large plantations oriented toward profit-making were important to the economy during the eighteenth century, and they were principally worked by African slaves supplied by English and other traders. The owners lived in cities in the mountain range running parallel to the coast from east to west, or in the Andean spur reaching deep into the region from the southwest. South of the coastal range and east of the Andes are the plains beyond which runs the muddy water of the Orinoco River. To the south of the river lies the forbidding jungle that stretches to the Amazon River.

VENEZUELA:
GROUPS

The mulatto descendants of planters and slaves preferred to escape the master-and-man relationship characteristic of the plantations and the discriminatory treatment of the cities by fleeing to the vast and treeless llanos, or plains. Mixing with the Indians and mestizos of this region, the mulattos joined them in cattle raising. Taking their name from the llanos, the *llaneros*, or cowboys, roamed free and careless, living to drink, gamble, and kill, always fiercely loyal to those demigods who commanded their loyalty as much because of their *machismo* and charisma as because of their prowess with the lasso and machete. The *llaneros* despised the way of life of the sedentary creole planters and deeply distrusted their ambitions.

The creole landowners were often at odds with the merchants despite their common style. The merchants who were most disliked were the commercial representatives of the Caracas Company, a monopoly enterprise organized under royal auspices in 1728. Its creation had been prompted by the mushrooming growth of contraband trade. Modeled on the East and West India companies of the English and the Dutch and opened to the investment and direction of enterprising Basques, the company policed the coast and drove away the smugglers, introduced new crops to diversify production, and returned profits reaching 20 percent a year. But the landowners were less than satisfied with the Caracas Company for it manipulated prices. When the company was finally forced to dissolve in the 1780s, it left behind a heritage of rancor.

Society in the cities was rigidly stratified. The landowners carefully maintained their distance from "inferiors." Insisting upon the purity of their own racial heritage, they were alarmed at any "uppity" behavior by *pardos*, or mixed-breeds. Racial feeling became particularly intense toward the end of the eighteenth century because an increasing number of *pardos* with industry and drive had achieved moderate wealth. Sometimes they even became the land-owners' creditors, causing further alienation. Racial tensions were further exacerbated by newly arrived Spaniards, who thought such attitudes ridiculous and proffered business opportunities and government posts to the *pardos*. The result was that the Spaniards and landowners were at logger-heads, and the *pardos* were their pawns.

The grievances were often vented in the *cabildos*, which enjoyed more prestige and exercised more power than other *cabildos* in Spanish America because the Spanish government neglected the area. This neglect encouraged the members of the *cabildos* to think that they were the arbiters of their own affairs. The existence of several cities of more or less equal wealth and the absence of a viceroy, leaving only a captain general to rule in Caracas, probably contributed to their sense of independence.

When the Bourbons ended this era of "salutary neglect" and began to tighten the reigns of command toward the end of the century, their actions were resented. Then the European wars at the turn of the century were a further irritation, for taxes were increased; French and English ships alternately raided the coast, according to Spain's shift-ing alliances; and workers had to leave the plantations to defend the coast. On the eve of independence Venezuela seethed with discontent.

MEXICO:
REGIONS

The Viceroyalty of New Spain, stretching from Oregon to Central America, was the shining star in the Spanish im-perial firmament. New Spain had a population of 6.5 mil-lion, which was more people than any other viceroyalty, and was also the most prosperous one.

At the center of New Spain, both topographically and politically, lies Mexico City, embedded in a delightful valley at an altitude of almost 8,000 feet and enjoying perpetual spring. Northward from this valley stretch two ranges in a somewhat lopsided V. The western range merges with the Rocky Mountains; the eastern range is shorter and ends around Monterrey. Sixteenth-century adventurers had dis-covered rich silver mines in the mountains where the V becomes narrower and around Mexico City. Northwest of

Mexico City is the city of Guanajuato, the center of one of the most prosperous areas in Mexico. Fabulously productive silver mines had been discovered in the hills about the city; its population had grown to sixty or seventy thousand. South of Mexico City the knotty mountains dissolve in strands that separate tropical valleys. Along the Balsas River and in the hot humid plains that stretch to the Gulf of Mexico were the sugar, cacao, and tobacco plantations, which added to Mexico's export wealth and helped diversify her economy. Imports flowed in legally from Spain through Veracruz and illegally from other countries through every cove and sleepy harbor on the Caribbean coast. These goods then competed with those produced by craftsmen in highland cities, such as Puebla. On the Pacific coast, Acapulco was the terminal point of a rich trade with the Philippine Islands; Mexican silver was sent in exchange for silks and other oriental products.

**MEXICO: GROUPS** Mexico's prosperity produced marked social tensions, for some groups and individuals were on the rise, while others were in decline. At the top of the social pyramid, as elsewhere in Spanish America, were the Spaniards. Mexico's wealth attracted a large number of them to administer the bureaucracy that channeled revenues to Spain.

Below the Spaniards were the creoles, and there were several important distinctions among them. One group may be characterized as *nouveau riche*. These were creoles who had recently accumulated staggering fortunes. Frequently they were only one generation removed from Spanish immigrants, but they had succeeded through great energy, ambition, and important contacts.

Another group of creoles, often in decline, were the descendants of the conquistadors. These creoles had rested too long on the glories of their antecedents and had paid too little attention to cultivating their inheritance. Nevertheless, they desperately clung to the vestiges of their former position, and one of these was often a proprietary seat on a *cabildo*. They were inclined to the professions, especially law, for through its practice, without dirtying their hands, they could maintain appearances. They also entered the clergy or became teachers.

The next group of creoles was the upwardly mobile petite bourgeoisie. These were storekeepers, small land-owners, businessmen, administrators for absentee landlords, government employees, and parish priests in the more im-poverished areas, who had enough wealth and education to desire a better deal, but not enough influence to secure it. Not far below them in social position were the artisans, occupants of the very lowest government positions, such as postal clerks and night watchmen, and the unemployed who would rather beg from better-placed relatives than rub shoulders with the castes.

The castes were those who were obliged to pay the tribute, or head tax. Although it is meaningless to speak here of race in any scientific sense, they were thought of as being Indians, blacks, or the result of race mixture. Some mestizos paid the tribute and some did not, thus intensifying the restlessness provoked by unsure status. Members of the castes were tried by separate courts, not allowed to carry weapons or own horses, exempted from certain taxes and from the tithe, and restricted by sump-tuary laws. Some creoles probably felt that this last pro-vision unduly circumscribed the consuming market.

The Indians in the central valley of Mexico and the re-gion south of Mexico City, the area of pre-Columbian high civilization, had been allowed to continue village life much as it had been at the time of their conquest. The only immediate change was that they were compelled to pay to the king's appointed delegate the tribute levied on each village collectively according to the number of males in a specified age bracket. Centuries of attrition changed the ancient villages. The chieftains became the creatures of the Spanish; the sexual appetites of the whites who passed through villages (despite royal prohibitions) diluted the racial stock, and the visits of the parish priest cast a new layer of form and meaning over the old religious practices; but the Indians still dressed in traditional clothes, spoke their ancient languages and preserved the bedrock of their spiritual life. Their dependent status made them easy prey for whites, and they usually did as they were told by the priest, landowner, or merchant with whom they were most likely to be in contact.

In the area around Guanajuato, however, the situation was quite different. This area had never really been Aztec territory, and village life was much more easily disrupted by the Spanish presence. The wealth of the mines and the heightened demand for food had also tended to destroy the ancient relationships of man to land and of men to each other. The Indians understood Spanish or even spoke it. They were part of an active money economy, and they were aware that they were not fully participating in the prosperity of the region.

In the northern ranch country the life of the Indians was even more affected by the Spaniards; they were cowhands and peons, kept in a lowly position and ignorant of their particular identity. Not far from them, in the hills of the northwest and the plains of the far north, Indian tribes, almost entirely untouched by the Spanish presence, still roamed free. Many of these Indians were more ferocious than at the time when Coronado first explored that area more than two centuries earlier.

Thus Mexico included many diverse elements. Not only were there the two broad categories of the ambitious and the satisfied, but the ambitious saw their future in diverse ways. The *nouveau riche* hoped for increased wealth under a system monopolized by themselves; the mestizos wanted to participate more fully in the wealth-producing opportunities. The Indians hoped for little but revenge.

*       *       *

The diversified economy of Mexico meant that all regions would profit from closer contact with the industrial centers of Europe. The coastal planters welcomed smugglers; the mine owners were glad to get more for the product; and the *nouveau riche* and petite bourgeoisie felt the future lay with them and that closer European contacts would be good. Since Venezuela became prominent only as the expansion of the European economy stimulated plantation agriculture, it too would gain by more liberalized trade with northern Europe. On the other hand, and not surprisingly, Spanish merchants in Mexico and Venezuela frowned equally on such a prospect.

The promise of a modern society had a more varied appeal. Mexican creoles were too much aware of their past traditions and their life was too closely identified with the corporate society to abandon it that easily, so the intellectuals' influence was relatively limited. Venezuelan creoles saw no conflict between the modern world view and their aspirations, so the new ideology spread more easily.

Venezuela and Mexico were most similar in the intensity of class feeling. Although the social structure of Venezuela was less complicated than that of Mexico, the friction between creoles and less favored groups was the same. The *pardos* of Venezuela and the mestizos of Mexico desired a more open society in which social mobility would be easier. The more acculturated Indians in the region around Guanajuato apparently felt the same way, but those of more traditional Indian villages accepted their dependence and subservience without much question. Class friction was to play an equally large part in the struggles for independence in Mexico and Venezuela, but in almost opposite ways.

# Chapter 4

# Satisfaction
# with Colonial Status

Peru and Bolivia are extremely different from Brazil. The towering Andes have no counterpart in the geological formation of Brazil. The Spaniards had found the Indians in the Andes highly civilized creators of complex and indigenous civilizations; while in contrast the Portuguese had found the Indians in Brazil so uncivilized that they had been forced to import vast numbers of African slaves to supply the labor of the colony. The only similarity between the two areas is that the creoles in both colonies were equally satisfied with their colonial status.

PERU AND BOLIVIA    The coastal area of Peru is arid, but along the snow-fed rivers which flow to the Pacific, haciendas had been established, worked by African slaves and Indian laborers. The chief crops produced on these estates were grains, cotton, and sugar, but the area was not Europe-oriented. Most production supplied only local demands and those of the highland mines because Europe was far away and exportation difficult from Peru's location. So in Europe tropical products from the Caribbean undersold the Peruvian ones.

The wealthy landowners lived in Lima, which was an aristocratic, Spanish-oriented, commercial town with no roots in Indian tradition. Silver from the mines was exported through the adjoining port of Callao, and before the trade reform of 1778, all legally imported manufactured goods from Europe that were destined for southern Colombia, Ecuador, interior Peru, Bolivia, Argentina, and Chile also passed through the port. There were some craft shops, but most textile weaving was carried on in the northern city of Cajamarca. Lima, being a seat of a viceroyalty, was also the center of a Spanish bureaucracy, and many of its residents were Spaniards.

That Lima was one of the centers of Enlightenment thought in the last part of the eighteenth century is just one more proof that ideas alone did not make the revolutions of Spanish America. A whole generation of articulate liberals was trained at the Real Convictorio de San Carlos, a college-seminary created after the expulsion of the Jesuits in 1767, but the goal of these intellectuals was reform, not revolution. This limited program may be a tribute to their realism, for there were no groups in Lima to benefit from independence. Export markets were of no interest. The legal restrictions upon commerce benefited the chief personages of the city, and independence could only restrict the orbit of their economic power. And the creole aristocracy preferred the glow of viceregal splendor and the ancient tradition of colonial preeminence to the crass authority of *arriviste* presidents.

The highlands of Peru and of Alto Peru, today Bolivia, were chiefly populated by Indians of ancient civilization and depressed status, many of whom labored virtually without pay in the silver mines. Sometimes the Indians revolted. One of the most spectacular revolts was the rebellion of Tupac Amaru in Peru in 1780. José Gabriel Condorcanqui Noguera, despite his mestizo origin, claimed descent from an Inca (that is, king). He had acquired an education and became incensed at the plight of the Indian masses. Assuming the name of the last known Inca, Tupac Amaru, he called for a general rebellion in the highlands to force reform. Bloody massacres followed in which the Indians vented upon their white oppressors the rage they had contained for centuries. But Tupac Amaru hesitated to attack the city of Cuzco, an essential target, and the Spanish authorities, recovering from their initial surprise, put down the Indian uprising within six months. Punishment was wreaked with unrestrained violence. The arms and legs of Tupac Amaru were tied to four horses, and he was torn apart. After peace had been restored, pardons were issued, and some attention was temporarily given to ameliorating the condition of the Indians. The rebellion had little further significance except to frighten creole men of property away from any revolutionary inclinations they might have otherwise developed.

The cities in the highland regions, where a small Spanish-speaking minority ruled over the mass of Indians, were not seriously stirred by any talk of economic injustices imposed upon them by the Spanish system. Closer contacts with northern Europe were of no interest. Curiously, however, the city of Chuquisaca (today Sucre) was the site of a university with a surprisingly advanced curriculum. The modernizing spirit implicit in Enlightenment ideas made rapid advances, and some leaders of the independence movement in Buenos Aires were trained there.

But regardless of the ideas of a few intellectuals, the basic position of the Andean region was one of satisfaction with colonial status. Neither Europeanization nor modernization was attractive. Only military force brought in from outside was to effect the independence of these areas.

BRAZIL: REGIONS     Although Brazil is not cut up by towering Andean ranges, its vast size has exerted almost as divisive a force as the more spectacular topography of Spanish America. The oldest area of settlement was a narrow strip of land running from the tip of the northeastern bulge southward beyond Salvador and ranging in width from 50 to 100 miles. This area is characterized by a generally rolling terrain, a humid climate, and a rich soil, and the land was divided into huge sugar plantations where thousands of African and sometimes Indian slaves labored in the fields and in the mills. The masters, however, did not typically resort to sumptuous living in the cities; they preferred the placid existence of the country, where, as lord of the manor, they held overwhelming power over the slaves, their families, and other dependents. From 1550 to 1650, this region was the major supplier of sugar to the world. When mines were discovered to the south at the end of the seventeenth century, the landowners lost their position at the center of the Brazilian economic and political stage. Although a century later they regained some of their former economic importance, they never regained their political importance because the re-vitalized Portuguese bureaucracy curtailed them. The hinterland of this coastal strip was a semiarid region, sparsely inhabited by ignorant cowboys devoted to cattle raising.

The area to the north and west of the bulge played a very small role in determining the course of affairs. Aside from a momentarily vigorous cotton production in the province of Maranhão, this whole area was only marginally related to the international economy. Because of prevailing winds, communication between this area and the rest of Brazil was difficult, and for long periods, the area was separately administered.

The connection between the sugar coast and the south was closer, not only because of the sea, but also because the São Francisco River, which runs through the center of the hinterland, flimsily linked Salvador and Recife to the area of "General Mines," or Minas Gerais. At the end of the seventeenth century vast resources of gold and diamonds were discovered there, rapidly upsetting the regional, economic, and social balance of the entire colony. Planters and slaves abandoned everything and flocked to the region. Others came in such numbers from overseas that the Portuguese government, fearing depopulation, was forced to prohibit emigration. Around the placer mines large towns grew up overnight, overshadowing the older cities. The turbulent, socially mobile existence of these newcomers shattered old relationships. After the middle of the eighteenth century the mines played out, and the area entered a period of economic decline. The fact that so much of the mineral wealth had gone to Portugal either as taxes or as profits to Portuguese merchants made this area the scene of some discontent. An abortive conspiracy was even organized in 1789 to declare independence and establish a republic. Although supported only by a handful of conspirators, the move was symptomatic of local sentiment.

The mines had been discovered by mestizo explorers emanating from São Paulo. Driven by economic and psychological necessity, other restless, ambitious, foot-loose men had then extended Portuguese control over the bulk of the area that is now Brazil, despite the legal rights of Spain. At the end of the colonial period the inhabitants of São Paulo were still proud of their role in handing over to the king such vast areas and great treasures and were still resentful of the scant appreciation they had been shown in return. The regions they had opened up had been cut away from their jurisdiction, the wealth they had discovered had fallen into the hands of new arrivals from other parts of the country or from Portugal, and their free-and-easy style of self-government (or anarchy) had been circumscribed by the imposition of more stringent governmental institutions.

The discovery of the mines had drawn the political center of gravity southward, and in the 1760s the capital of the entire colony was relocated from Salvador to Rio de Janeiro. By the beginning of the nineteenth century Rio de Janeiro was the most important town on the Brazilian coast, profiting from its position as chief entrepôt for the legal and illegal commerce of the mining region. Despite its beautiful setting among green hills and sandy coves, the town of Rio de Janeiro was a backward provincial capital, beset by disease and characterized by muddy, filthy streets. Even the elevation of the colonial governor to the titular position of viceroy had not done much to give Rio de Janeiro the luster of Lima or Mexico City.

To the far south, in an area long disputed with the Spanish, lay the grasslands of Rio Grande do Sul. Life here resembled life in Uruguay or Argentina much more than life in Minas Gerais. Yet its inhabitants conceived of themselves as Brazilians and remained so perhaps because of the smooth process by which independence was achieved.

BRAZIL: GROUPS  The creole* landowners were satisfied with their colonial status, for the Portuguese were relatively lax in administration, and the elite had a great deal of political power to add to their wealth. They not only ruled unchecked over

---

* For the sake of simplicity, I will use the familiar term "creole" to refer to any person of Spanish and Portuguese descent born in America despite the fact that in Brazil the equivalent term *crioulo* meant a black born in America.

their vast properties, but they also dominated the *câmaras*, or municipal and county governments. In an enlightened effort to create a national state and end once and for all the vestiges of medieval times, the Portuguese government, ably directed by the Marquis of Pombal, began in the eighteenth century to trim the wings of local *câmaras*. But the new program was not enforced overnight, and the irritation of creoles remained minimal. Furthermore, the Portuguese were not as restrictive as the Spanish regarding commerce, so there was little real difficulty in exchanging Brazilian products directly for goods from northern Europe.

Nonetheless, restrictions existed, and the beneficiaries were the Portuguese merchants in the coastal towns. Excluded from immediate landownership because of their late arrival and initially limited resources, and refusing to work as farm hands alongside slaves, Portuguese immigrants had tended to concentrate in commerce. Landowners scorned this activity and were at first successful in preventing the merchants from sitting on the local *câmaras*. But, as the Portuguese merchants prospered, they became the creditors of the landowners, and real animosity sprang up between the two groups. If the children of these immigrants decided to stay in Brazil, they bought plantations themselves or foreclosed on mortgages and moved as quickly as possible to disassociate themselves from the activity of their fathers. More often, the immigrant or his son returned to Portugal to enjoy the fruits of hard labor and the rewards for enduring the scorn of the planters. The merchants naturally wanted the government to intensify the restrictions laid upon trade with foreigners. They also cherished their monopoly of government contracts for the equipment of the navy, the collection of taxes, or the supply of stores to government establishments. The colonial relationship was dear to them.

By the end of the eighteenth century a small lower middle class had gathered in a few cities. This class was easily stirred up against the aloof and haughty merchants. Caught between the upper grindstone of Portuguese predominance and the nether one of cheap slave labor, this class was irritable and tense and, therefore, volatile. In 1798 mulatto tailors and common soldiers, stirred up by a priest and a

Latin teacher, launched an unsuccessful revolt in Salvador.

The chief manipulators of this class were the urban intellectuals, inspired by the ideals of the Enlightenment and devoted to the inclusion of their country in the main currents of the Western world. But their importance must not be exaggerated. There were not only few issues to play upon, but also few intellectuals. There was no university or institution of higher education in all of Brazil, and few could afford to study in Portugal. Furthermore, as there was not a single printing press before 1808, the effectiveness of the intellectuals in spreading the new world view was greatly limited. If it had not been for extra-Brazilian events, decades probably would have passed before the intellectuals could have mobilized enough favorable opinion to create an independent Brazil. The processes of modernization had made scant progress in Brazil.

\*     \*     \*

The scarcity of innovating intellectuals suggests the real similarities between Brazil and Peru and Bolivia despite obvious differences. In these regions those excited by the Enlightenment found few cracks of elite dissatisfaction in which to wedge new ideas, for the creoles had few reasons to complain. With the exception of abortive revolts stimulated by fringe elements in Bolivia, Minas Gerais, and Salvador, independence came to both areas from the outside and was not formalized until the 1820s, a full decade after independence movements began elsewhere.

# Chapter 5

# European
# Events

Political agitation in Spanish America began in 1808 when news arrived of Napoleon's usurpation of the Spanish crown and took on real impetus as his armies became more successful. The independence movement enjoyed victories and suffered defeats until the restoration of King Ferdinand VII in 1814, after which the movement suffered mostly defeats until the culmination of military victory in 1824. The independence movement in Portuguese America was entirely different, but related events in Europe brought about a similar result. When Napoleon invaded Portugal in 1807, the king actually fled to his American domain, which made Brazil, in a sense, independent, but not completely free of Portuguese control for another two decades. Any attempt to understand the story of independence must begin in Europe and then turn to the reactions of the Americans.

SPAIN AND FRANCE 1788–1805

The "enlightened despot," Charles III of Spain, died just a year before the French Revolution broke out. His successor, Charles IV (reigned 1788–1808), was well-meaning, but stupid, and did whatever his wife wished. At middle age her fancy turned to romance with a handsome twenty-five-year-old officer in the palace guards. Manuel Godoy (1767–1851) was of petit bourgeois background; he thought he was a liberal, but he was primarily an opportunist. As the queen's favorite, Godoy was rapidly promoted not only into her bedchamber but also to the post of chief minister of the realm. Charles IV gave him full powers over domestic and foreign policies, and Godoy became a mean and petty dictator. The old aristocrats were outraged at this climber's success, and the reformers were appalled to see such a charlatan pretending to their principles.

With the leftward swing of France after 1789, Spanish leaders became steadily more frightened. Spain abandoned its historic enmity toward England and joined her in the First Coalition against France. By late 1793, however, the coalition began to fall apart. The end of the terror in France and the assumption of power by the more conservative Directorate assuaged Spanish fears and made an alliance with England anachronistic. A treaty of friendship between France and Spain was therefore signed in 1796. When Russia and England formed a Second Coalition against France in 1798, Spain preferred to side with France, and England, whose navy completely controlled the seas, retaliated by cutting off Spain from her American colonies. The year before the Spanish government had officially sanctioned colonial trade with friendly neutrals; and although this trade was envisioned to be with the United States, it was the British who reaped the greatest advantage from such liberality. This was a taste of economic independence. When the measure was revoked two years later, English vessels continued to ply the Spanish coast in the Caribbean, in the Río de la Plata region, and on the west coast of South America. Thus the economic independence of the colonies was being forged long before political independence became a live issue.

The alliance between France and Spain continued after Napoleon's rise to power. In 1801 he played upon the silly pride of fawning Spanish royalty by promising to give a kingdom in Italy to the daughter of Charles IV in exchange for that part of Louisiana which Spain had been granted at the conclusion of the Seven Years' War. Then French armies joined Spanish ones in attacking Portugal, England's protegé. Portugal yielded part of its own territory to Spain and allowed French Guiana to expand southward to the mouth of the Amazon River. A further threat to annex all of Portugal resulted in the signing in 1802 of the Treaty of Amiens between France and England. According to its terms England was allowed to keep Trinidad, which it had captured from the Spanish in 1797 and had consistently used as a base for clandestine trade with Spanish America, and France was left with its new territories in Louisiana and Brazil, both controlling access to continental river systems and both well situated in relation to the Caribbean. But Napoleon's refusal to accept the British demand for a cessation of his expansionist activities on the Continent was unsatisfactory to the British, who declared war the next year.

Napoleon was taken by surprise. He now concentrated on Europe. Louisiana was hastily sold to the United States, and despite Spain's disappointment in this act, she was persuaded to declare war on England. For Napoleon had decided to invade England and needed additional Spanish ships to transport men and equipment across the channel. The French and Spanish fleets were hounded into port at Cádiz; when they attempted to break out, Lord Nelson decisively defeated them off Cape Trafalgar in 1805.

SPAIN AND
ENGLAND
1797–1807

If Napoleon could readily discard or postpone his overseas ambitions, British policy makers faced a more difficult choice: Should they concentrate on colonial conquests, leaving the Continental war to their allies? Or should they concentrate on defeating the French in Europe, in the face of their allies' failure of will and inability to fight to the end? Instead of making a firm choice, the British pursued an ambiguous policy that did much to foster independence sentiment in Spanish America but not enough to accomplish independence.

The difficulty of resolving this dilemma was not only strategic but political and economic: The business community was in desperate straits. The newly mechanized factories were producing more products than the markets were able to absorb. The years of war with France had broken old commercial ties on the Continent, and the Treaty of Amiens had failed to restore them while it had simultaneously curtailed trade in Spanish America. If the Spanish colonies could be captured, the business community would have a sure market and the government would have a secure source of bullion to finance the allies. But England lacked the resources for a massive colonial war; the only alternative was to encourage revolution, for the English had not forgotten the American Revolution; nor had Francisco de Miranda.

Miranda (1750–1817) was born in Venezuela and went to Spain as a young man to join the army. He fought against the British in the American Revolution. Although he did not think much of the United States, Miranda somewhere absorbed liberal ideas and a belief in colonial freedom. He eventually abandoned the Spanish army and roamed Europe seeking support for his schemes to free Spanish America. He found that the London business community and also the naval captain Sir Home Popham were interested in his schemes. Popham introduced Miranda to his influential political friends, which ultimately led to semi-official conversations with William Pitt. These conversations resulted with a plan to invade Venezuela with a few thousand troops. But the plan was abruptly halted when Pitt was persuaded that Spain could still be won away from France and included in a Third Coalition. Miranda in disgust departed England and headed for the United States, and Popham was dispatched to capture the Cape of Good Hope before it could become unfriendly territory. Neither man forgot the possibility of liberating Spanish America.

Miranda, doggedly determined to carry on without British support, obtained two hundred men and sailed out of New York for Venezuela in January 1806. He was so completely out of touch with affairs in his home country that he thought his mere appearance off the coast of Venezuela would result in an uprising. Instead, when he landed in April, the local inhabitants stared at him uncomprehendingly, and Spanish forces quickly routed him. Miranda sailed for the West Indies where he secured the promise of support from the British Admiral Thomas Cochrane. Thus encouraged, Miranda tried again without success. The British cabinet received the news of his attempts at the same time it was trying to arrange peace with France. An attack

on Spanish colonies seemed ill-timed, but the cabinet instructed Cochrane to send "full details of the situation in
which the Continent of South America now stands." *

Meanwhile, Popham became bored with his duty of
patrolling the Atlantic around the Cape of Good Hope.
He heard that Napoleon had smashed the Third Coalition
at Austerlitz in December 1805. Since this assured Spain's
loyalty to France, Popham assumed that Pitt had given him
authority to take such measures against the Spanish as he
and Miranda had once imagined. In April 1806, Popham
set off for the Río de la Plata region with a part of an
army garrison commanded by William Carr Beresford to
capture either Montevideo or Buenos Aires. News that
Buenos Aires had just received a shipment of silver from
the interior decided in its favor. The city was captured
almost without effort. But a creole militia, led by Juan
Martín de Pueyrredón, drove the British out of the city in
August.

Beresford in the meantime had sent home, not only news
of the initial success, but also over $1 million in booty,
which was paraded through the commercial section of London in September. The merchants were electrified. In 1805
their exports to Spanish and Portuguese America had
amounted to more than $38 million; they felt that if this
trade could be relieved of the frightening fluctuations
which accompanied its illegality, there was no telling how
high the figure would reach. The merchants rushed to
send out goods to Buenos Aires on consignment and pressured the government to support their enterprise with
guns.

Some members of the British cabinet had been advocating
a more forceful Latin American policy. Now, as had not
been the case with Miranda's adventure, a British force
had been successful, even if unauthorized, and must be
supported. Also Napoleon's victories and his decrees closing
Europe to British trade affected the decision. So a military
force was sent out to reinforce Popham, and plans were

---

* Quoted by William Spence Robertson, *The Life of Miranda*,
2 vols (Chapel Hill: University of North Carolina Press, 1929),
vol. I, p. 318.

made for attacks on Panamá, Chile, Peru, the Philippines, and Mexico.

Inefficiency, red tape, and the difficulty of preparing concrete plans delayed action; then, in January 1807, news arrived that Buenos Aires had been surrendered the previous August. The grand plan was reduced to concentrating on recapturing Buenos Aires. Furthermore the defeat indicated that the Spanish-Americans were not eagerly awaiting their deliverance from Spain. Yet even in this modest aim the British were unsuccessful. Although an army of ten thousand men was dispatched to Buenos Aires, it was met with fierce house-to-house combat in which the British suffered a thousand casualties and lost two thousand prisoners. A truce was struck, and by September 1807 the defeated British were on their way home.

PORTUGAL
1807–1808

News of this defeat reached London only a few months before the announcement of Napoleon's pact with the Russian Czar at Tilsit. Napoleon now dominated practically all of Europe, and he intended to enclose the remainder. He was furious at Portugal for not closing its ports to British trade even though he knew that his armies were often dependent on British goods smuggled through those ports. In mid-August 1807 Napoleon demanded that Portugal declare war on England and join the Continental system. For Portugal there were three alternatives. One was to yield to Napoleon's demands. However, if Portugal declared war on England, that would be the end of her domination in Brazil because England controlled the sea. Another possibility was for Portugal to join England. However, England demanded that Portugal remove her restrictions upon British penetration of the Brazilian market —the British economic plight was intensified by Napoleon's closing the European ports—and that the Portuguese court be moved to Brazil for safety. The third possibility was for Portugal to delicately play France against England, desperately trying to save through sophisticated diplomacy what Portugal's limited military capability could not hope to safeguard. Negotiations were spun out so that Napoleon's ultimatum requiring compliance by September 1, 1807, was not carried to its conclusion until late November. In the meantime Portugal attempted to persuade England to agree to a false declaration of war, but England found this duplicity distasteful and was too anxious to get the Brazilian trade to play that game. At the beginning of November Portugal began to comply outwardly with Napoleon's demands while keeping England informed of every step.

However Portugal carefully outlined another course of action in case these steps failed. This contingency plan was to move the court, government, and accouterments of government to Brazil. Every detail was foreseen. Ships were surveyed and charted for available space; a line of command was established; papers were selected; treasury accounts were put in order. But no overt action was taken because any sign that the government was indeed planning to flee, as the British desired, would have provoked an invasion. Only one problem could not be overcome: Portugal's small size meant that an invasion would be known in Lisbon only four days before French armies would arrive at the city. The Portuguese gambled that this would be long enough to carry out the massive task of removing, not just the sovereign, but the entire machinery of government. They won that gamble. Only the sails of the ships were visible when Napoleon's officers reached the quay in November 1807, four days after the French army had crossed the border.

The careful planning that enabled the Portuguese government to escape French domination is all the more impressive because the court in Brazil was to be not simply a government in exile, but a new empire. The large number of people who fled Lisbon is partly explained by this factor. Fifteen thousand Portuguese crowded into ships that had been prepared for one-third that many. The crossing of the Atlantic was not easy. The escorting British ships could not prevent the onslaught of a storm, and the vessels were scattered and greatly delayed. Food and water ran short. By the time the Portuguese arrived off the Brazilian coast in early 1808, the ladies were forced to shave their heads to rid themselves of lice; the wives of the Brazilian planters who flocked to the port thought this must be the latest fashion in Europe and hastened to do likewise. On arrival in Brazil, the Portuguese government's first action was to throw open the ports of Brazil to the trade of friendly nations. British merchants now had at their disposal a market of two million people to be clothed with cottons made in British mills. Napoleon's action had done more for British businessmen than Popham's or Miranda's.

**SPAIN**
**1807–1814**

Thus encouraged, British leaders looked once again at the prospects in Spanish America. In early 1808 Arthur Wellesley was charged with studying the military aspects of a campaign to liberate Venezuela. Wellesley concluded that conquest was out of the question, but that, if the Venezuelans desired it, liberation was within the realm of possibility. The British recalled Miranda from his virtual exile in the West Indies and assured him that at last his hopes were to be realized: Britain would free Spanish America from Spanish "oppression." But his hopes were soon destroyed.

Napoleon decided to take direct control of Spain. He had already cajoled Godoy into allowing French troops to cross Spain to reach Portugal and had then established a corridor across Spain between France and Portugal. The old aristocrats continued to chafe at Godoy's crass behavior and looked to Prince Ferdinand, who was old enough to think for himself (which does not mean he did so), for salvation. When Napoleon demanded the right to occupy northern Spain, officers in the army, supported by a skillfully manipulated mob in the streets, successfully demanded the abdication of Charles IV. In May 1808 Napoleon lured both Charles IV and Ferdinand VII to southern France under the pretext of offering mediation, but instead he announced that Charles's abdication would hold and that Ferdinand would abdicate in behalf of Napoleon's brother Joseph Bonaparte. Offered the choice between a risky attempt at escape, perhaps to America, and the gift of an estate in France, Ferdinand chose the second.

No sooner did news spread that Ferdinand had been kidnapped than revolts broke out in Spain which drove Joseph from Madrid. Only massive military support from France was able to restore him to the capital. Then began the Spanish War of Independence. Like the wars that were subsequently to sweep Spanish America, it was also a civil war. Many Spaniards had always looked to France for their inspiration and felt that a new king could perhaps revitalize Spain as the Bourbons had done a century before. The Spaniards who thus collaborated with the foreigner were mostly moderate liberals. This collaboration with the foreigner helped discredit liberalism in Spain throughout the nineteenth century. The opponents of the French were either conservatives or ultraliberal nationalists and naturally fell to quarreling. This too was to become a characteristic of modern Spain.

Nevertheless, the French found it hard going. Juntas, or committees, were organized to direct defense efforts in each Spanish province and in each village. These juntas quickly turned to guerrilla warfare. The Spaniards were at their best in guerrilla warfare. This type of warfare puts a premium on individual action, courage, mobility, and the commitment of the population, and relies little upon organized discipline. Furthermore, guerrilla warfare puts a regular army to its hardest test because in its desperation, the regular army alienates the civilian population whose disaffection provides the basis for guerrilla success. Napoleon soon complained that Spain was like a running sore. Thousands of French troops were poured in to hold the territory that had been occupied, for as soon as a French army moved on to another target after capturing one locality, the Spaniards rose up again and fought from the rear. Still Napoleon did manage little by little to expand the area under his control.

The first British reaction to Napoleon's move on Spain was to think of Spanish America. Wellesley was appointed commander of an army to invade Spanish America. But when delegates from rebel juntas arrived in England and told of the fierce struggle that the French still faced, it seemed to the British that the best policy was to invade Spain. So Wellesley was sent to Spain. In such a situation it was impossible openly to encourage revolution in Spanish America; yet it was equally foolish to discourage it in case the peninsular campaign failed.

In September 1808 the various Spanish juntas sent representatives to a central coordinating committee in Seville, out of which developed the Central Junta. Two years later this junta was driven southward to Cádiz. The Central Junta dissolved later that year and was replaced by a regency. In quest of legitimacy (for Napoleon pointed to Ferdinand's signed abdication as the basis for his), this regency summoned a cortes, or parliament, to meet in Cádiz. Most members of the cortes were radicals. The liberals were collaborating with the French, and the conservatives were too attached to their properties or their responsibilities to run from the French. Only the radicals were free enough of material and moral encumbrances to flee to Cádiz. In their deliberations they were driven by the consideration that they must outbid Napoleon in their liberalism. The result was the Constitution of 1812, which established a constitutional monarchy that so restrained the power of the king that it was virtually a republic. By abolishing many of the outworn institutions of the old regime—the Inquisition, privileges of the nobility, feudal dues—these constitution makers uttered a cry of ultraliberalism which was to reverberate throughout Spanish America for more than a decade.

On only one issue did the constitution makers shy away from change: The colonies were to remain dependent. Cádiz was the very center of the monopoly trade which characterized colonial relations, and the local merchants were influential in the deliberations of the cortes. When the British demanded that the ports of America be opened, the Spanish replied that their efforts against the French were a sufficient quid for the British quo. Although the regency issued a call for delegates to the cortes from the colonies, it made sure that these delegates, even in the unlikely event that they all came and arrived in time for the deliberations, would be outvoted. In the absence of the colonial delegates Americans resident in Cádiz filled some of the American seats.

Meanwhile, the military struggle was beginning to go against the French. Wellesley's army slowly consolidated its hold in Spain and occupied more territory. At the end of 1812 the French armies were forced to retreat from Russia; the next year they suffered further defeats by a

Fourth Coalition of anti-French allies and were also driven out of Spain. In the spring of 1814 allied armies converged on Paris.

Napoleon released Ferdinand VII on the startling condition that he would restore the Spanish-French alliance. By the time Ferdinand occupied his throne in March 1814, there really was no Napoleonic government left. In May Ferdinand tore up the Constitution of 1812 and proceeded to persecute those who had collaborated with the French and the radicals who had dominated the cortes. He, like the French Bourbons, had forgotten nothing and learned nothing.

# Chapter 6

# Tracing Causes
# in Spanish America

The independence movement in Spanish America can be divided chronologically into two distinct wars for independence. The causes of the second war are easily found in the experiences of the first unsuccessful one and in the behavior of the Spaniards after the revolutionaries were defeated. The puzzle, then, is how the widely divergent regional and group reactions to the forces of Europeanization and modernization in Spanish America can be linked to the onset and course of the first war. This chapter will trace those connections by working backward from military action to the role of diverse interest groups, to the impact of ideas, and finally, to the nature of the constitutional crisis that confronted Spanish-Americans.

MILITARY  
FORCE

If Spain, in 1810 and the years immediately thereafter, had been able to marshal its full military might against the revolutionaries in America instead of dispatching only small reinforcements, events there might have been very different. In some areas, such as Peru, Spanish power during this initial period was never even challenged; in other areas local Spanish forces were sufficient for the task at hand. A small Spanish garrison, moving out of Puerto Rico, drew upon the enthusiastic support of creole royalists to sweep away the first independent government of Venezuela in

1812; Spanish armies, marching from Peru, expelled liberating Argentine soldiers from Bolivia in 1813 and crushed the revolutionary movement in Chile the following year. Evidently, a relatively small increase in Spanish power or an equally small decrease in insurgent strength might have eliminated all the foci of revolutionary action in America, prevented the drawn-out struggle that hardened attitudes and divided Americans from Spaniards, and maintained the Spanish Empire intact for perhaps another fifty years. Instead, the Spanish garrison in Venezuela was unable to subdue Colombia until reinforcements arrived from Spain in 1814, and the armies from Peru were not strong enough to move to Buenos Aires to snuff out the movement there. By 1816 the Spaniards were victorious, but they had taken too long and their success had been too incomplete. These two factors were crucial in provoking the second and successful war.

The chief opposition to the Spanish forces in 1810 and the years immediately thereafter was the creole militia officers. In Buenos Aires the creole officers, confident after victories over the British in 1806 and 1807, pressured the *cabildo* and the viceroy to create a local junta to rule in behalf of Ferdinand VII. In Chile the story was much the same. In Colombia the officers fraternized with the mobs that they were to disperse. The importance of the creole officers may be judged by the contrasting situation in Mexico: Instead of siding with the revolutionaries, the officers were the first to take the leadership in crushing them. The explanation is that an intellectual made the mistake of arousing the Indians to revolt; with all the property and established social relations in jeopardy, the creole men of wealth, the fathers of the officers, sided with Spain. If the creole officers had put down the revolutionaries in other parts of Spanish America, no movement toward independence would even have begun.

The ascendancy of the creole militia in Spanish America was short-lived, however. In Venezuela the creole officers were unable to command the loyalty of their troops, which were made up of slaves and mixed-breed pariahs. In Chile and Colombia the officers fought among themselves, opening the way for Spanish reconquest. But the point is that the creole militia officers successfully initiated the independence movement by using the force they commanded, successfully held off the Spanish for several years in much of Spanish America, and kept Argentina completely free of Spanish domination after 1810.

In view of the early importance of the creole militia officers, the position of the aristocracy from which they arose is of prime importance in explaining the onset of the independence movement, but the diversity of sentiment among the aristocrats exemplifies the complexity of Spanish America. Although it is probably safe to say that in every area there were some creole aristocrats who were willing to support independence, the strength of their feeling varied greatly.

In some regions the landowners' interest in independence was based on economic reasons. The planters of Venezuela, Mexico, and the northern coast of Colombia, and the ranchers around Buenos Aires knew that their products were consumed in northern Europe and that they would get better prices through direct sales. But there were other regions where the economic factor was relatively unimportant. The planters of Chile sent their products mostly to Peru and were free to send them to other ports along the Pacific coast or to Argentina, and the planters of the Colombian highlands distributed their products locally because the terrain prevented them from supplying the coast. None of these landowners was interested in direct exports to overseas consuming centers. Nor did the landowners in the valleys of Mexico have any particular desire to export to northern Europe. Thus the landowners in different regions were impelled as much by economic interests as by social theory to take opposite positions regarding independence.

Nor was the advantage of the lower cost of imported manufactured goods of equal interest to all consumers, although the aristocracy always supported steps which facilitated this importation unless it offended other of their interests. In Chile, for instance, where the planters were not much hurt by the old system, they were nevertheless willing to consider change. They received silver from Peru in exchange for their wheat, and this silver went farther when the prices of imports were lower. Similarly, the gold exported from Colombia paid for more manufactured goods when it was sent directly to England. The haciendas of highland Mexico supplied foodstuffs to the mining towns; the mineral wealth received in return went to pay for the expenses of sumptuous town houses which called for European imports. Even the hacienda itself required some tools and iron products which were best supplied from abroad. On the other hand, if the imported products competed in price with local ones, then the feeling was reversed. Thus the wine and sugar producers of western Argentina looked with disfavor upon measures which opened the east coast to foreign competition; however, these producers were in the minority. If landowners remained loyal to Spain, this loyalty was the result of other kinds of countervailing pressures. Most noticeable is the case of Mexico, where the landowners perceived much more advantage in maintaining Spanish power than surrendering to a maddened horde of Indians. And elsewhere it may be said that only when the desire for cheaper imports was combined with other interests—a desire for better prices on exports, lower taxes generally, or greater power locally—did the landowners get stirred up enough to fight for independence.

Among merchants, distinct divisions must be made between those who profited from the monopoly trading system and those who did not. The former were mostly Spanish-born agents of the large merchant firms of Cádiz. Even after the trade reform, large-scale legal commerce remained in the hands of these men. The establishment of *consulados* in Santiago and Montevideo symbolized the achievement of their maximum aims. Although the old established merchants, as in Lima or Veracruz, resented the increasing freedom granted by the Bourbon kings and imposed by the turn-of-the-century wars, they did not think independence would be better than the status quo. The most that can be said is that perhaps they were lackadaisical in defending a system which seemed to them already destroyed.

The men who bought from the old established merchants were the native middlemen. These small merchants were ambitious types, unreconciled to remaining forever in the shadow of the larger merchant houses, and were susceptible to the wiles of the contrabandist. When the leaders of newly independent countries moved to loosen the commercial system, lifting restrictions on foreign trade and ending many of the earlier monopolies, these merchants benefited and gave the new governments their support. This was true in Buenos Aires and in Caracas, and would have been true in the minor cities of Mexico (for example, Veracruz) had not the independence leaders there threatened the safety of all trade. It is interesting to contrast the position of merchants of western Argentina and Lima, who almost unanimously looked back nostalgically to better days, were far from anxious to transform Buenos Aires into a major entrepôt, and saw independence as a step in the same direction as the "disastrous" Bourbon reforms, with those in Mexico City, who, because of the greater vigor of its trade and the profits some had derived from Bourbon measures, violently disagreed among themselves as to whether independence would be good or bad.

The position of craftsmen before the threat or promise of independence has not yet been adequately studied. The competition of foreign imports would surely have strengthened their loyalty to Spain, but many of them derived more protection from the difficulties of internal transport than from legal rigidities. Textile shops in Puebla, Mexico, seem to have maintained that city on the side of Spanish power until 1820; but their counterparts in Socorro, Colombia, do not appear to have shared their loyalty. In some areas, as in southern Colombia, where craftsmen were important, one may ask whether it was direct economic interests or the highly traditional societal structure that contributed to the strength of loyalist sentiment.

Closely related to the question of trade, but in a sense overriding it, was the question of power. There is little doubt that the creole aristocracy desired power and wished to wrest it from supercilious Spanish bureaucrats. This ambition was linked to the issue of free commerce, because with power they could foster their own economic interests whatever they were. The fulfillment of this goal would also—and this is very important—give them the right to tax and disburse funds in their own behalf. Ironically, they believed that mestizos and mulattoes could then more easily be kept in their place, and also that the Indians could be further exploited, as indeed they later were.

IDEAS The role of the creole intellectuals assumes real importance once the position of landowner and militia is clear. Committed to change and knowing what they wanted, the intellectuals were quick to take advantage of a crisis whose origins lay in Europe, to play upon the economic or other interests of landowners and to manipulate the officers. In Peru the intellectuals' endeavors were a failure because of the entrenched conservatism of Spanish merchants, bureaucrats, and churchmen; in Mexico their entreaties also fell upon deaf ears because of initial tactical mistakes; but in Argentina, Chile, Venezuela, and Colombia, the intellectuals were successful primarily because they expounded a well-elaborated ideology of modernization.

This ideology was the Enlightenment. The Spanish government considered the new doctrines then sweeping Europe as dangerous and subversive to the established order. But the government's effort to prevent the penetration of these ideas proved a chimerical goal, for ideas have a life of their own. Once any Spanish-American had had contact with the new critical approach, nothing could prevent him from thinking subversive thoughts and even infecting others.

Antonio Nariño (1769–1822), a somewhat quixotic Colombian intellectual, demonstrates the conclusions to which the Enlightenment could lead. In 1794, he translated and published the Declaration of the Rights of Man, apparently unaware of the effect this would have upon a government fast becoming jittery over the regicidal behavior of French revolutionaries. Nariño had the curious idea that he could make money from this editorial venture despite the fact that he had to print it in the secrecy of his home. The Spanish authorities seized him, and after imprisonment, shipped him off in chains to Spain. In the port of Cádiz, however, he escaped his ship as it was docking and proceeded disguised through Spain to France and then to England. Nariño then trustingly returned to his native land, where he was promptly clapped back into jail to be released only in 1803 for medical reasons. He was then required to remain on his landed estate, under virtual house arrest.

Preventing the distribution of a translated Declaration of the Rights of Man was one thing, but preventing the spread of its ideas was quite another. Literate men were bound to discuss these ideas whenever they met. Furthermore, many societies had been formed with royal approval both in Spain and in America for the purpose of propagating novel agricultural techniques, stimulating economic activity, discussing industrial possibilities, and exploring the applicability of newly discovered scientific principles. The intellectuals who organized such clubs in Spanish America and who published or wrote for periodicals to expound and popularize these new ideas found that, in order to change economic conditions and transform Spanish America into a progressive, scientifically oriented, and entrepreneurially active society, basic changes were needed in the social structure and political organization. For these intellectuals, it was not possible to speak of progress without casting a new look at tax structures, commercial restrictions, and monopoly agents. Inevitably, Spanish authorities disbanded the societies, confiscated the periodicals, questioned the leaders, and made other attempts to foster "clean" societies.

At first most of the intellectuals would have been satisfied with reform. If Spain had granted more local autonomy in 1810 or 1812, perhaps the intellectuals would not have pushed the movement to independence; but Spain did not, and independence became their goal. Although the intellectuals' subsequent efforts fell far short of a genuine social revolution, they were not entirely without fruit in moving Spanish America closer to the mainsprings of Europe. The patterns of society and economy were far different in 1830 than in 1808. This result was partly due to the influence of ideas.

CONSTITU-   The ideas of the intellectuals would have been in vain, or
TIONAL CRISIS  at least long-delayed in their effect, if it had not been for the unsettling events that overtook Spanish America entirely without local effort: In Europe Napoleon usurped the Spanish throne. This event created a crisis because of the preexisting constitution of the Spanish-American government. Conceivably, Spanish-Americans could have continued to obey viceroys, *audiencias,* and intendants; and they

could have received instructions from the Seville junta and subsequent regency; but, although this policy was adopted in some places, it was rejected in most because Spanish-Americans did not consider themselves colonials. Napoleon had removed their *own* king, usurped his throne, and left them entirely without a government. Without a king, where did one's loyalty lie? The ties that bound a man to his own home were the only other worthwhile emotional commitment. With the king gone, only the immediate locality was left. Thus the regionalism that has so often been decried as the tragedy of the Spanish-American wars of independence was, in fact, their very root.

When the Spanish failed to recognize the validity of this regionalist sentiment and attempted to enforce their rule, the creole elite resisted. The intellectuals provided justifications and suggested alternative forms of government that could be useful, and the militia provided the necessary armed force. Except in Mexico and Venezuela, the resistance that followed in other areas was not a war aimed at independence with a considered program and definite goals. A commitment to such a program was in most places hewed out during the course of warfare against "illegitimate" Spanish pretenders and years of self-governing experience. Meanwhile, new groups that had never been heard from before had emerged to prominence and had to be taken into account. The old system could certainly not be reimposed on them. So the causes of the Second War of Independence (after 1814) are different from those that were operative from 1808 to 1810. An examination of the two struggles for independence in each major area of Latin America will give concrete meaning to these general considerations.

# Chapter 7

# The
# First War
# of Independence

The First War of Independence was directly provoked by the constitutional crisis in Spain. Creole intellectuals, or segments of the population interested in modernization and Europeanization, or both, seized control of the juntas that were set up in most of Spanish America to deal with that crisis. These leaders, momentarily successful, began to establish closer trading connections with northern Europe and/or more modern institutions at home, but they were soon defeated by internal divisions and crushed by Spanish forces. Spanish power was reimposed on all Spanish America except Argentina and Uruguay. Yet despite the defeats that marked the conclusion of the First War of Independence, it is the more important war, for the first war clearly established the issues and created the sentiments that were to prove decisive in the second war. It also exposed the terribly sharp internal divisions that have been typical of Latin America ever since.

ARGENTINA The British invasions of Buenos Aires in 1806 and 1807 encouraged the Europeanization of the Río de la Plata region. Landowners, ranchers, small merchants, and intellectuals were excited by the possibilities opened up by direct commercial connections with England and the rest of Europe, and the alleviation of customs dues further emphasized the burdensome nature of Spanish rule. Moreover, the creoles were encouraged by the militia's victory over a well-trained and experienced army and by the choice of their own viceroy, Liniers, when the Spanish appointee fled. Therefore, the British invasions are justifiably looked back upon as a turning point in the road toward independence in Argentina.

The Spanish government did not send out a replacement for Liniers until mid-1809. The delay was caused by the crises in Spain. The new viceroy arriving in Buenos Aires was named not by the king, but by the Central Junta of Seville. His claim to rule was based on the theory that these American provinces were a part of Spain, not merely joint kingdoms under a common crown, and that the Central Junta was therefore the only legitimate representative of the king. The new viceroy's most immediate task was to solve the economic problem. Since Spain was largely occupied by foreign troops and the normal channels of trade were closed, the landowners, ranchers, and small merchants stridently demanded that in the present crisis they be allowed to trade freely with all countries. The intellectuals readily provided for their use reasoned arguments based on Enlightenment thought. The viceroy yielded, despite the protests of the Spanish merchants, and opened the port to non-Spanish shipping.

In May 1810 the news arrived in Buenos Aires of the collapse of the Central Junta and most of the legitimatist forces in Spain. A *cabildo abierto* was convened. Pressured by a mob incited by political activists, the participants in the *cabildo* decided to depose the viceroy, now without claim to a mandate, and to organize their own junta to govern in behalf of the captured Ferdinand VII. One of the earliest acts of the junta was to remove the remaining restraints upon European trade.

Although ready to unite behind the issue of trade, the leaders in the junta were deeply divided on most other issues; these divergencies began to emerge at once. The leader of the junta was Cornelio Saavedra, a conservative who opposed efforts to transform the ideological and sociological foundations of the established order; but he was outnumbered by Mariano Moreno, Manuel Belgrano, and Bernardino

Rivadavia, liberals who wished to break ties with the make-shift Spanish regency. They also moved to institute reforms in trading regulations and in the relationship of church and state and to establish secular schools and a free press. Opposed to such modernization, Saavedra resorted to the expedient of seating on the junta delegates from the interior cities, most of whom, of course, were conservative. The enlarged junta forced the resignation of Moreno after seven months in office—he died of natural causes shortly thereafter—and conveniently dispatched Belgrano to enforce the hegemony of Buenos Aires over Paraguay, a task for which he was unsuited by temperament and training.

The new junta, rid of most of its more liberal members, lost much of its political support and proved to be too cumbersome for effective action. In September 1811 the junta named an executive triumvirate to rule with a rotating membership, but its policies continued to be inconsistent. In the meantime the triumvirate's modernizing secretary, Bernardino Rivadavia, accrued increasing influence and actually served as triumvir. Under his direction steps were taken to put a final end to the slave trade, to encourage immigration, and to reorganize the judicial system. The triumvirate also crushed an attempted counterrevolution led by a prominent Spanish merchant. The triumvirate was overthrown in 1813 by a combination of dissident elements because of its failure to satisfy either liberals or conservatives and its adamant refusal to bow before the will of a constituent congress. Another constituent congress was soon convoked, which once again ran aground on the shoals of conservatism and basic disunity within the body politic. Then by carefully screening the delegates from the interior cities, a liberal representation was obtained for this congress; and it quickly proceeded to abolish the Inquisition, terminate titles of nobility, discard the practice of entailment, and declare that henceforth all children born of slave mothers were free. At the beginning of 1815, the congress appointed a young liberal, Alvear, as chief executive, labeled supreme director; however, the congress avoided a declaration of independence, precisely to skirt the issues of monarchy and centralism.

The erratic and arbitrary actions of the self-seeking Alvear coupled with his liberalism-cum-centralism led to his overthrow by discontents who relied upon the power of the Uruguayan caudillo José Gervasio Artigas (1764–1850) for support. By this time Artigas was at the head of a loose confederation of five hostile provinces to the north of Buenos Aires. The conservative groups in Buenos Aires now appealed to the interior provinces for political support against the liberals and summoned another constituent congress to meet, not in Buenos Aires, but in the interior city of Tucumán. It met in May 1816, and its actions form part of another chapter in the independence movement.

URUGUAY When news arrived in Montevideo of the usurpation of the Spanish throne in 1808, the leaders of Montevideo immediately began to quarrel with those of Buenos Aires. They accused viceroy Liniers, who had been chosen by the leaders of Buenos Aires, of being pro-French, a traitor to the Spanish crown, and therefore unworthy of their loyalty. They formed their own junta with the Spanish governor in Montevideo at the head. The junta was voluntarily disbanded when Spain sent out a replacement for Liniers. In 1810 the junta of Buenos Aires, which claimed to govern in behalf of Ferdinand VII, asked for the adherence of Montevideo; the latter refused, declaring its loyalty to the Spanish regency, which also ruled in the name of the king. Then Spain named another viceroy for the region and made Montevideo the viceregal capital instead of Buenos Aires. Thus, Uruguayan independence from Buenos Aires overshadowed independence from Spain.

Then Spanish officials began to use Montevideo as a base of operations against the new government in Buenos Aires, and many creoles in Montevideo became uneasy. Furthermore, the leader of the Uruguayan gauchos, Artigas, defected to the side of Buenos Aires and began a lightning campaign against the Spaniards in Montevideo, which reduced the area under Spanish control to the limits of the city itself. The Spanish viceroy appealed for help to the Portuguese monarch in Rio de Janiero, who sent in an army. Faced with the Spanish forces in Montevideo and the slowly advancing Portuguese army in the interior of Uruguay, the Buenos Aires government signed a truce in late 1811 agreeing to let the Spanish viceroy control all of Uruguay. The Portuguese retreated under British pressure. Inconsolable, Artigas and four-fifths of the population of the hinterland of Uruguay retreated to the Argentine province of Entre Rios, where they remained for more than a year before returning to continue the fight against the Spaniards.

Meanwhile, Artigas' relations with Buenos Aires deteriorated. He sent delegates to the congress called by the liberals in 1813 and there demanded a federative government with local autonomy for the provinces. Since this congress failed to grant him what he wanted, indeed, failed to seat his delegates, he turned against it and fought both the Spaniards and the *porteños* simultaneously.

When the restoration of Ferdinand VII appeared imminent, the government in Buenos Aires became desperate to rid the Río de la Plata region of Spanish rule. Montevideo served as a lodestone for Spanish forces invading from Bolivia and also offered a beachhead for armies dispatched from Spain. The government in Buenos Aires enlisted the support of William Brown, an Irishman, who, commanding a makeshift fleet, blockaded Montevideo from the sea. The residents of Montevideo actively aided the Spanish in their efforts to defeat the *porteños;* but in June 1814 the city surrendered, and Buenos Aires again controlled it. Then Buenos Aires attempted an unsuccessful domination of Uruguay; Artigas recaptured Montevideo in early 1815. He instituted as enlightened a government as could be expected in such years of crisis while he expanded his power in northeastern Argentina.

CHILE   Chile was ruled at the time of the usurpation of the Spanish throne by an adinterim governor. The events in Europe encouraged the intellectual creoles who desired independence to speak out against his ineptitude, which brought upon them his uncontrolled and distemperate wrath. The governor's overreaction only widened the intellectuals' circle of adherents among the creole aristocracy, who already distrusted the Spaniards' loyalty to the king. Of course, the Spaniards in turn suspected the creole aristocracy of lacking loyalty to Spain and accused them of wishing to rule themselves in guise of loyalty to a deposed king. When the governor heard that the Central Junta in Seville had collapsed and that a junta had been formed in Buenos Aires, he moved with special severity against three leading creoles of Santiago, banishing them to Peru. This action resulted in open protests. The *audiencia* forced the resignation of the governor in July 1810.

The next man in line for the governorship was in his dotage, but the *audiencia* supported him, hoping that his Chilean birth would satisfy the creoles and that his age would make him easy to manipulate. The creoles, however, were more adept at using him than the Spaniards were, and he agreed to summon a *cabildo abierto*. The Spaniards did not appear, either because they were not allowed by the creole militia to enter the hall or, more probably, because they did not wish to undergo the humiliation of being outvoted at such a gathering. The *cabildo abierto* accepted the resignation of the new governor and named a junta to rule in behalf of the king.

The junta moved immediately to win political favor by instituting some reforms, convoking a national assembly, opening trade to all nations, and organizing a military force. The national assembly, which convened in July 1811, was controlled by moderate and conservative creoles, who wished to limit their actions to some reforms, to send delegates to the Spanish Cortes, and to stop short of any radical alterations in the status quo. But another group in the assembly, smaller but more liberal, wanted to declare independence and establish a republic.

One of the liberal leaders in the national assembly was Bernardo O'Higgins (1778–1842), the illegitimate son of the Irish-born viceroy of Peru. He was partially educated in England, where he met Francisco de Miranda and acquired some of his ideas. When his father died, O'Higgins inherited considerable properties in Chile and returned there in 1802, a man of substance, but with seditious ideas.

Alongside O'Higgins in spirit, although not a member of the national assembly, was the lawyer Juan Martínez de Rozas (1759–1813). He had once been a legal adviser for Bernardo's father and had subsequently held positions of authority, but his creole origin frustrated his desire for preferment beyond a certain level.

Another liberal leader in the national assembly was the political economist Manuel de Salas (1755–1841). He was more interested in increased autonomy than in outright independence; his opinions carried much weight.

When the national assembly named an executive committee to rule while a constitution was being drawn up, not one of the liberals was included. They resigned in protest. Their resignation stirred to action the three Carrera brothers, Luís, Juan, and José, sons of one of the wealthiest and most influential creole families in Chile. Luís, Juan, and their father had been active in the protests against the governor; José had been in Spain at the time as an officer in the Spanish army. Upon his return to Chile, José became fully committed to independence. He was dismayed by the moderate tenor of the national assembly and by the predominance in it of another wealthy creole family. When the liberal members resigned, he determined on more forceful action. Winning over elements of the creole militia, he led a coup d'état which purged the national assembly of the more conservative leaders and introduced a majority of liberals.

The new national assembly proceeded immediately to modernize the old institutions. It abolished the Inquisition, created a single national court system and educational system, and declared free the children born of slaves. By interfering in the system of parochial fees, putting parish priests on a fixed salary, and creating secular cemeteries, it began the long struggle between church and state which characterized the next century of Chilean history. This national assembly was short-lived, and many of its reforms were quickly undone, but it accomplished the task of spelling out in practical measures the implications of the Enlightment.

José Carrera soon decided that, if one coup d'état had worked so well, two would be better; he dissolved the assembly and created a triumvirate with himself at the head and O'Higgins as another member. Tired of this arrangement, he led still a third coup d'état and placed himself in sole command. He introduced a series of reforms, among them setting up the first printing press, decreeing the establishment of primary schools in every town, and combining three seminaries of Santiago into the National Institute.

But other liberals were offended by Carrera's arbitrary methods and by aspects of a family feud which he had introduced into the struggle. Civil war broke out between the forces which he led and those commanded by O'Higgins and Martínez de Rozas. The regionalism, so characteristic of Spanish Americans, also came into play since both men were from the southern province of Concepción and opposed efforts by Carrera to rule the entire country from Santiago.

These petty quarrels laid the groundwork for a larger crisis. The viceroy in Peru dispatched a Spanish force by sea to southern Chile, and, marching northward from there, the Spanish force met Carrera's forces at Concepción, which was captured in March 1813. Carrera's alleged mismanagement of the campaign brought about his deposition and temporary replacement by O'Higgins. O'Higgins moved to strike a truce with the Spaniards, for he preferred a *pro forma* declaration of loyalty to Spain and the election of representatives to the Spanish Cortes to continued bloody military encounters. Carrera, however, was outraged and led his fourth successful coup d'état. Although their quarrel was momentarily patched up, Carrera's rancor led him at a crucial moment to refuse reinforcements to O'Higgins, who with his army was forced to flee over the Andes to Argentina, where he joined the army of General José de San Martín. The Spanish army proceeded to conquer and was in control of Santiago by October 1814.

VENEZUELA Venezuela was the first Spanish colony to be informed of the usurpation of the Spanish throne. A French agent was sent to Caracas to demand the allegiance of the colony. He was met with a cold reception from the captain general and a hostile mob commanded by creole militia officers. However, when the officers requested permission from the captain general to form a local junta as in Spain, he temporarily threw them into jail for their audacity. Later, when news arrived of the collapse of the Central Junta of Seville, the officers initiated their plan without the cooperation of the captain general, whom they deposed in April 1810, formed a junta, and immediately worked to establish its power. The junta deported the captain general and the members of the *audiencia,* successfully solicited the support of most of the other cities in the region, opened the ports to world trade and granted preferential tariffs to the British, and dispatched diplomatic missions to London and Washington to seek at least tacit support. Simón Bolívar was one of the diplomats sent to London, and there he recruited on his own initiative the support of Francisco de Miranda, who returned to Caracas with him. Bolívar and Miranda elaborated an ideology and pressed the congress, which the junta finally convened in March 1811, to declare independence. The American Confederation of Venezuela was created on July 7, 1811, making Venezuela the first independent country in Spanish America.

The act of declaring independence was unfortunate. The revolutionaries, scions of the landowners and educated in a European intellectual milieu, in their desire for independence did not know how far they had outdistanced the majority of the population, even many in their own class; they also forgot how near Venezuela was to the Spanish stronghold in the Caribbean. Many Venezuelans who would have been placated by a declaration of loyalty to the king considered the act as equivalent to cursing God. Under the current social order, this act was suicidal. Those who would have supported the idea of a junta modeled on the one in Seville were puzzled or dismayed. The *pardos* were distressed. The creoles, who had oppressed them the most, were in control; the property qualification for voting made it very clear that this movement was not theirs. The Spanish officials and clergy, who had been more solicitous for their welfare and had often ignored the silly prejudices of the creoles, were out of control. Therefore the Spanish found it easy to enlist the support of the *pardos;* and the revolutionary army, which by necessity was made up of *pardo* draftees and slaves marshaled by landowners, was plagued with desertions.

The Spanish garrison from Puerto Rico, which landed in the loyal northwestern part of Venezuela in 1812, had little trouble in gathering support and advancing rapidly toward Caracas. Despite the hurried elevation of Miranda to generalissimo and virtual dictator, nothing could stem the advancing Spanish-loyalist tide. Miranda capitulated and tried to escape with the treasury, presumably to fight again as he had done before, but Bolívar put another interpretation on this act and turned him over to the victorious Spanish in exchange for a safe-conduct for himself to Colombia.* There he pondered his past experience and planned for the future.

*Bolívar*    Simón Bolívar (1783–1830) has emerged as the great hero of Spanish-American independence. A native of Caracas, he was the son of a wealthy creole who owned two cacao plantations, three cattle ranches, thousands of slaves, and thirteen houses. He received his earliest education through a well-read tutor who was so thoroughly impregnated with the ideas of Rousseau that he made *Émile* his guide for the boy's instruction; then in 1799 he was sent to Spain to complete his education. The wife he married there died within a year, and he swore he would never remarry; he kept his promise, although it is said that he sired over one hundred children. In Europe Bolívar traveled widely and lived in Paris when Napoleon was in his glory. He moved freely within high society, enjoyed the gay Parisian pleasures, and studied Napoleon's military campaigns. Many of his observations were later utilized in his own campaigns.

Bolívar returned to Caracas and joined the creole officers who were expressing political discontent in 1810. He idolized Miranda and was anxious to enlist his support for the cause when he was sent to London; but after their return to Caracas, Bolívar became disillusioned with his hero. Miranda's apparent betrayal of the cause in 1812 prompted him to turn in his erstwhile idol before he fled to Colombia.

Colombia was in political turmoil when Bolívar arrived there. He tried to persuade the new insurgent government

---

* The name Colombia was first coined by Bolívar for a country he created from parts of the Viceroyalty of New Granada, which included approximately what is today Venezuela, Ecuador, Colombia, and Panamá. By 1830 it had dissolved into its constituent segments as we know them today, although Colombia itself was known as New Granada until 1863. We shall use the name "Colombia" in its present sense and refer, as do other historians, to Bolívar's chimerical creation as Gran Colombia.

that it would not be safe from Spanish authority until Venezuela was freed. The government refused to heed his warning; Bolívar disobeyed its orders and led a successful campaign against the Spaniards in eastern Colombia. When he returned bearing treasure, he was not court-martialed, but promoted to general.

Bolívar continued to dream of returning to Caracas in glory. After much pleading, the insurgent government gave him five hundred men to undertake an expedition in 1813. He moved eastward with lightning speed, repeatedly engaging the Spaniards before they realized he was near, and was in Caracas within three months. His campaign was a procession of triumphs against great odds, unparalleled since the days of the conquistadors; it was also a great learning experience for him. During the campaign he perfected his ability to command and experimented with propaganda. He virtually created the public manifesto, now so traditional in Latin America, and developed the triumphal entry to win over the masses. His great carriage was drawn by dozens of pretty girls through flower strewn streets. The crowds went wild with adulation.

Bolívar's campaign had by no means completely crushed the Spaniards in Venezuela. They by now perceived the division in Venezuelan society over the issue of independence and managed to enlist the full support of the *llaneros,* who were ready to fight against the hated city types and the haughty creoles. José Tomás Boves mobilized the *llaneros* for the Spaniards. Boves was a sadistic Spanish adventurer who had been arrested for smuggling by the creole government. He was released by the Spaniards when they took over in 1812 and immediately offered his services to them in exchange for booty. Boves had long been familiar with the ways of the *llaneros* and, by being more cruel than they were, he had won their respect. Eventually ten thousand *llaneros,* almost all on horseback, were at his command. In addition he had obtained the loyalty of the blacks and mulattoes by promoting them over the lighter skinned officers in his command.

Bolívar was no sooner in possession of Caracas than Boves loosed his hordes against him. Striking more swiftly than Bolívar and outdoing him in forcefulness, Boves was soon successful. Bolívar's troops began to melt away. By mid-1814 Bolívar was once more in flight; the class divisions of Venezuela had defeated him.

COLOMBIA There was relatively little reaction in Colombia to the usurpation of the Spanish throne. The legitimacy of the viceroy was not in question since he had been appointed by the king. He accepted the authority of the Central Junta of Seville and had relatively little difficulty in quelling an abortive revolt in Quito the following year. But, when news arrived of the collapse of the Central Junta, the viceroy's power began to wane. The *cabildo* of the coastal city of Cartagena demanded and secured from the local governor the right to participate in his decisions, and the leading citizens of Bogotá demanded that the viceroy summon a *cabildo abierto*. He was forced to comply when the creole militia defected from his camp. Inspired by the lawyer Camilo Torres (1766–1816),* the *cabildo abierto* organized a supreme junta in July 1810. The junta declared loyalty to Ferdinand VII, but would not surrender its right to govern unless he came to govern in person. The junta called a constitutional convention with representatives from all provinces and instructed it to create a charter to include a federal system in which provincial autonomy would be protected.

Jealousies immediately arose between Bogotá and the other Colombian cities, with Cartagena spearheading the opposition. The next year the supreme junta in Bogotá, admitting reality, called a local congress to draft a constitution just for the surrounding province of Cundinamarca. The junta also invited representatives from the other provinces to draft a pact between the acknowledged sovereign provinces. The representatives met, formed a congress, and in November established a very loose confederation, the United Provinces of New Granada, but it made no formal declaration of independence.

Some in Bogotá, however, were unwilling to make concessions to the regionalist feeling; among them was An-

---

* Not to be confused with the late revolutionary Colombian priest by the same name and of the same family.

tonio Nariño, who had emerged from house arrest in 1810. He insisted that unity was essential if Colombia was to withstand the onslaught of Spanish power and demanded that Colombia form a strong central government. When his preachments fell on deaf ears, he decided on more forceful action. Leading a coup d'état in Bogotá, he tore up the provincial constitution and proceeded to conquer neighboring provinces. Many of his officers resigned in protest and joined the forces of the beleaguered victims. Nariño meanwhile assumed increasingly dictatorial powers in the province of Cundinamarca and became steadily more unbalanced. Under his frantic leadership Cundinamarca seceded from the United Provinces of New Granada in the name of centralism.

The Spaniards took advantage of this internal political turmoil and mounted an offensive against the insurgent provinces, forcing Nariño and the United Provinces to agree to cooperate militarily. The war went badly, however; Nariño was captured in 1814, the local royalists in the northern city of Santa Marta revolted and reestablished Spanish control there, and the provinces began to fight among themselves once again. Then the congress of the United Provinces decided that the province of Cundinamarca must be forced to join the union. At this moment Bolívar returned from Venezuela after his second defeat and was given this task. He occupied Bogotá at the end of 1814. He next turned his attention to driving the Spanish out of the north, only to discover that Cartagena would not cooperate, partly for fear of losing its hoard of military stores and partly because of personal jealousies. Disgusted, he left Colombia and retired to Jamaica. In May 1816 Bogotá fell, and by August all of Colombia was back in Spanish hands.

ECUADOR,
PERU, AND
BOLIVIA

The rest of Spanish America was hardly touched by the First War of Independence. Groups of modernizing creole intellectuals established abortive juntas in La Paz, Bolivia, and Quito, Ecuador, as early as 1809 and later hatched unsuccessful plots in Lima, Peru. An armed rebellion in Cuzco, Peru in 1814 and 1815 was equally unsuccessful. Invading revolutionary armies, recruited in Argentina, momentarily liberated southern Bolivia, but these initial victories were deceptive. When one revolutionary general summoned the chiefly Indian population of Bolivia to hear his victory statement, he was met with sullen silence instead of the delirious cheers to which he had become accustomed on the plains. None of his allusions to liberty, to the rights of man, to the end of oppression met with a response. Finally, in desperation, the general asked, "What can we do for you? What do you want?" With one voice, the Indians boomingly replied, "*Aguardiente,* señor!" ("Firewater, sir!") * The Spanish could evidently supply more firewater; the plainsmen were soon driven off. Two more attempts, one led by Belgrano, were made to conquer this mountainous region; both were failures. These areas of traditionalism had not yet been excited by the promise of modernization and stood to gain nothing from closer contacts with northern Europe. The First War of Independence by-passed this region.

MEXICO  When news arrived in Mexico of the abdication of Charles IV in 1808, José de Iturrigaray, the viceroy appointed by Godoy, was afraid that he would be stripped of his lucrative position, for the Spanish community in Mexico City not only despised him as an unworthy representative of the mother country, but also suspected him of siding with the French as Godoy had. In the hope of securing his position, Iturrigaray summoned a joint meeting of the *audiencia* and *cabildo;* but when no consensus emerged, he sided with the *cabildo* in its demand for a local junta and consented to head the junta, apparently believing that this would make him more secure than if the junta in Spain were obeyed. Satisfied with his cleverness, he proceeded to rule as if nothing had happened. The creoles were momentarily satisfied, but the Spaniards were outraged and successfully carried out a plot to seize Iturrigaray. The *audiencia,* privy to the plot from the beginning, met and named a new viceroy. The Spaniards were in control again. The attempt at revolution from above thus ended ignominiously.

Nothing more happened in almost two years to suggest

---

* John A. Crow, *The Epic of Latin America* (Garden City, N.Y.: Doubleday, 1946), p. 460.

the momentous events that were next to overtake Mexico. As events in Spain, however, moved toward the defeat of the patriot forces there, secret societies and clandestine meetings of dissident creoles became increasingly common in Mexico. One group of conspirators, meeting in Querétaro, planned a coup d'état for December 1810; but in their efforts to secure support, they approached some who exposed the plot to the Spanish authorities. The plotters, warned of their imminent arrest, scattered and hid except the creole Miguel Hidalgo y Costilla.

*Hidalgo and the Mob*     Miguel Hidalgo y Costilla (1753–1811) was a parish priest. He was not particularly devout —he was, in fact, rather profligate. He had a good education, was interested in the ideas of the Enlightenment, and was deeply concerned with the plight of his parishioners, the Indians around Dolores. He had been banished there by the Inquisition because of his religious irregularities and dangerous ideas. The majority of his parishioners were living under subhuman conditions. Although the production of grapes and the cultivation of mulberry trees for silkworms had been forbidden in America because of the competition such activity gave to the merchants in Spain, Hidalgo knew that the law had been violated in some places. Therefore he encouraged the Indians to undertake these ventures and also helped them to establish a brickyard, pottery, and tannery. The companionship of ignorant Indians, however, was not enough to satisfy the roving curiosity of a well-read man who also enjoyed good living. He sought out like-minded fellows in nearby Querétaro and was brought into the conspiracy plot. Evidently he was not the driving force behind the plot, but when the others scattered, he decided to carry out a modified plan on his own.

At dawn on September 16, 1810, Hidalgo summoned the people to the parish church. Addressing them in their native tongue, he pointed out their miserable condition and blamed the Spaniards for it. He simultaneously declared his loyalty to Ferdinand VII, whom the Indians had been taught to venerate, and accused the king's subordinates of being untrue to their master. "Down with the Spanish! Down with bad government!" The Indians scurried to assemble machetes, pikes, clubs, and axes and followed him to the next village where a similar scene took place. "Long live the Blessed Virgin of Guadalupe!" became their cry as they appealed to the particularly Mexican, particularly Indian, madonna. Then to still another village marched the throng. Within a few days Hidalgo was at the head of a mob of several thousand, including some mestizos and a few creole plotters who hastened out of hiding. An attempt to transform the inchoate mass into a disciplined force failed. Since supplies were scanty, the mob raided haciendas, consumed crops and cattle, and also drew away the workers as new recruits. Then the mob tackled towns, plundering the shops, sacking the houses, raping the women, and smashing the machinery of mines and craft shops. When the mob invaded Guanajuato, the bloodshed was unrestrained and the destruction of property devastating.

It was a war of revenge against centuries of oppression. Although a few creole intellectuals in Mexico City continued to defend Hidalgo, most people of substance and education considered him a madman. Hidalgo did little to stop the mob, for he understood their frustration and sympathized with their outburst. When he realized the effect their destructive campaign was having on others, however, he began to have doubts himself, and his creole companions were appalled. They had hoped for a rebellion, not a social revolution.

Nevertheless, he moved toward Mexico City, leading some eighty thousand men. After a bloody day-long battle, his mob drove back the Spanish military contingent of twenty-five hundred soldiers sent out to defend the mountain passes surrounding the city. Then, on the brim of the valley, Hidalgo changed his mind and directed the mob to turn away from Mexico City.

The reasons for Hidalgo's decision are still disputed. Some historians claim that his sensitive soul recoiled at the thought of witnessing another scene of pillage and bloodshed; and some historians have suggested other reasons: The plan for an immediate rising of creoles, stimulated by initial victories won by the castes, might have worked if Hidalgo had been able to launch an effective propaganda campaign making clear his goals—if he had any—and appealing for the creoles' support before the gory details about Guanajuato had reached their attention. But he lacked a printing press, and the royalists had several. They distributed thousands of handbills throughout the major cities describing the bloody ravages of Hidalgo's horde. The creoles became alarmed and turned the illiterate Indians of the valley of Mexico, who were to have been more recruits, against him. Furthermore, Hidalgo knew that a large Spanish army was descending on the city from the north. If he were to invade, his followers would turn to looting and drinking and be easy prey for the advancing army.

Turning back was the end of the movement despite one more battle in which maddened Indians tried to stop the Spanish cannons with sombreros. The battle was lost when a magazine exploded and the resulting grass fire spread terror in the ranks. The Spanish soldiers moved in ruthlessly. Some adventurers fought on, but the first phase of the Mexican war for independence was over. Hidalgo headed north to Querétaro and eventually was betrayed, tried, and executed on July 31, 1811. He had settled nothing, but he is remembered as the first hero of Mexican independence.

The effort so far was more akin to the rebellion of Tupac Amaru in Peru than to the other struggles for independence in Spanish America. The long pent-up hatreds of the Indians gave impetus to both Hidalgo's movement and the former one. Well-educated leaders intent on reform rather than revolution and inspired at least partially by the new thought of the Enlightenment lit both sparks. The leaders hesitated to invade major cities, the capture of which could have paved the way to final success. And in both cases the movements frightened men of property away from any thought of revolutionary solutions to their problems. But timing often gives a meaning to historical events which is not built into their logic. It was the thought of independence which sparked the activity of Hidalgo, and this purpose was read into his movement by both friendly and hostile observers. This meaning was picked up and borne further by his immediate successors. The social significance of the movement, as opposed to the political message, only affected the effort adversely and was not hailed for at least another generation.

*Morelos and the Guerrillas*     Hidalgo's work toward independence was not entirely in vain. One of his lieutenants who continued to fight was José Maria Morelos (1765–1815). Morelos, trying to rise within the lower middle class, had entered the seminary where Hidalgo was the rector before his banishment to Dolores. Upon completion of his studies, Morelos was appointed the priest for the hot humid valley of the Balsas River. When he heard about Hidalgo's mad adventure, he rushed to join his ex-teacher, who told him to return to the Balsas River valley and foster revolution there.

In this task Morelos was more successful than his mentor because he was a skillful organizer and a man of perserverance. Depending on peasants who could be fierce fighters one moment and peaceful tillers of the soil the next, he proceeded to conduct a large-scale guerrilla warfare that intimidated the creole landowners and destroyed the system of Spanish control in the southern regions of Mexico. He soon attracted financial support from those who wished to be on the winning side. He increased the size of his guerrilla army by appealing to political conviction. He advocated complete racial equality, the abolition of the *fueros*, the breaking up of the large estates into small holdings, the abolition of the compulsory tithe, the seizure of church lands, and other radical reforms designed to bind the loyalty of the masses. By the beginning of 1813 he had an army of nine thousand men, supplied with captured Spanish weapons, and was in control of all of Mexico south of Mexico City, Puebla, and Veracruz, except Acapulco. He soon acquired sufficient power and influence to convene a congress (of eight members) to draft a constitution. Meeting in Chilpancingo, the congress declared Mexico independent on November 2, 1813. It then concentrated its attention on legal questions that perhaps should have been postponed. Bickering was the inevitable result. By the time the constitution was ready the next year, Morelos had lost most of the territory once under his command.

Morelos' biggest mistake was that he did not move upon the capital when he could have done so. By the beginning of 1813, when he was at the height of his power, he was in contact with an active fifth column within Mexico City, made up of lawyers, government employees, and other professional men, who had organized an effective intelligence and propaganda organization. The viceroy reported in desperation that it informed the revolutionaries on "the status of the forces, munitions, and supplies, all of which [information] is taken from the offices of the government; accounts of the resources of the government, its scarcities and its difficulties." * This group urged Morelos to move on Mexico City, assuring him that his name was now a byword and would enlist immediate support. But he failed to follow their advice. Instead, he spent the entire summer besieging Acapulco—apparently in a quixotic determination to carry out instructions received from Hidalgo three years earlier—while the Spanish army smashed the strongholds of his allies and left him isolated. The government then undertook a vigorous counterinsurgency program in the south: All propertied creoles were provided with arms on the gamble that they would not be used against the government. By the end of 1813 Morelos began to suffer his first defeats, which continued for the next two years. Finally, the Spaniards encircled his last position and overran his fortification. He was executed on December 22, 1815.

With Morelos gone, the independence movement did not long survive. The remaining leaders fought among themselves. Spanish forces consistently searched out and emptied the pockets of rebellion. By the end of 1817 practically the entire country was at peace. The revolutionary leaders were either captured and executed or retired to private life, accepting pardons or disguising their identity. Although a few bandits were still at large, cloaking their activity with the banner of independence, only two men of genuine patriotism continued in rebellion. Holed up in the hills, virtually hermits, Vicente Guerrero in the west and Felix Fernández, alias Guadalupe Victoria, in the east, continued to dream of independence for Mexico.

BRAZIL  The complete independence of Brazil was secured gradually and almost imperceptibly over a period of twenty-three

* Wilbert H. Timmons, *Morelos: Priest, Soldier, Statesman of Mexico* (El Paso: Texas Western College Press, 1963), p. 86.

years from 1808 to 1831. During this time, events in Europe overtook Brazilians and impelled them along a course which they had hardly considered before 1808. Of the European events that set the pace, the most important were the French invasion of Portugal and the removal of the court to Brazil in 1807 and the defeat of Napoleon in 1815. One may confidently maintain that in effect Brazil was independent by 1815, although Brazil celebrates 1822 as the date of independence.

The arrival of the Portuguese court and government in Rio de Janeiro transformed Brazil's status from an obscure colony to a seat of government. The new government speeded up the process of Europeanization and modernization. The ports were opened to the trade of friendly nations, namely, England; industries were encouraged; a national bank was established; and a new judicial system was instituted. The king gave Rio de Janeiro a sophistication which it had never known because the splendor of viceroys had escaped it; it was now amply rewarded with the pomp and ceremony of a genuine European court. Furthermore he directed the foundation of a medical school, a national museum, a national library, and a botanical garden. The royal press became Brazil's first printing establishment.

When Portugal was liberated from Napoleonic rule, King John VI was naturally expected to return, but he preferred to stay in Brazil. To solve this awkward problem, he elevated Brazil to the legal status of kingdom, making Rio de Janeiro his capital. Thus Brazil achieved by 1815 a goal that Mexico was a long way from attaining. A revolution from above, tried so fleetingly and unsuccessfully in Mexico in 1808, succeeded easily in Brazil. Of course, the assumption of power by a viceroy cannot compare in significance with the arrival of a king and court, and, indeed, this disparity suggests that if the Spanish king had fled to Mexico, that nation's history might have been much more like Brazil's.

\*      \*      \*

Social revolution and political independence appear to be antagonistic. In Mexico violent class warfare pointed the

way toward social revolution, but it failed to produce political independence, indeed, hampered its emergence;
whereas in Brazil social relationships remained virtually unchanged, but political independence was achieved without
the use of force. One tentative conclusion to be derived
from this juxtaposition is that the crisis of legitimacy in
Mexico provided the opportunity for the emergence of social violence. On the other hand, that crisis does not explain
this phenomenon because the slaves in Brazil would probably not have risen up against their masters as the Indians
did in Mexico. The use of a comparative approach thus
serves to highlight the complexity of the historical process.

A comparison between Mexico and Venezuela reveals
that class division was a powerful inhibitory effect on political independence. In Mexico the creoles' fear of social
revolution stymied political independence; whereas in Venezuela the lower-classes' fear of creole dominance halted
political independence.

A comparison between Venezuela and Argentina reveals
that, in spite of common interests in Europeanization and
modernization, their experiences were different. Venezuela,
unlike Argentina, was closer to the stronghold of Spanish
military bases in the Caribbean, and therefore, the independence movement was easily subdued. Venezuelan leaders,
unlike Argentine leaders, made the error of declaring independence rather than insisting on loyalty to the king; thus
they alienated many who might have supported the more
limited goal of a local junta ruling in behalf of the king.
The preexisting class hatred in Venezuela far exceeded the
animosities between gauchos and urban residents in Argentina; and although friction between these groups in Argentina increased, no Spanish forces were in a position to take
advantage of them as they were in Venezuela.

A comparison between Argentina and Chile reveals several points at which their experiences resembled each other.
Creole militia officers, supported by mobs, forced the formation of local juntas and the deposition of weak and demoralized Spanish administrators. Creole intellectuals—
Moreno, Belgrano, and Rivadavia in Buenos Aires and
O'Higgins, Martínez de Rozas, and Salas in Santiago—
played a prominent role in the initial proceedings. However,

in both areas conservative forces arose to ease out the liberals. Since the liberals did not hesitate to use force to regain their earlier position, civil war ensued. Out of this chaos arose a new phenomenon: *caudillismo*. Artigas on the east coast and the Carreras on the west exemplify it. Regionalism was an important factor in their success. However the results were different in each place. In Chile Spanish forces defeated the revolutionaries and reoccupied the country; whereas in Argentina they were driven out. The reason for this development was the limitations of Spanish military power and the relative location of the two countries: Spanish armies from Peru could more easily reach Chile than Argentina.

In 1816 only relatively isolated Argentina, Paraguay, and Uruguay were free of Spanish control. Elsewhere, regional rivalry, class hatreds, and divided leadership so weakened the revolutionary cause that by using small military contingents already in America in 1810 plus limited reinforcements from Europe after 1814, the Spanish succeeded, with the help of loyalist creoles and revengeful lower-class elements, in crushing the revolutionary forces.

The most important result of the First War of Independence was the creole experience of power. The creoles also gained a sharpened awareness of the differences between their interests and those of the mother countries. The power they sometimes exercised was naturally used to advance their distinct interests, especially to facilitate commerce with northern Europe. One of the first acts of practically every junta was to open the ports to British vessels.

Creole intellectuals advanced some aspect of the modern world view in all areas. In Chile and Argentina specific reform legislation was enacted. In Venezuela and Colombia the fighting, either with the Spanish or with other creoles, was too intense to allow much time for the elaboration of a reform program. In Mexico the attempt to reform society alienated the very groups that might otherwise have cooperated in more modest goals. In Brazil the Portuguese government imposed some traces of modernization. Thus, although independence was not everywhere won, it was now recognized as a means toward larger goals and established as an ideal in a large part of Latin America.

# Chapter 8

# The
# Second War
# of Independence

There were two principal causes for the Second War of Independence. One was the First War of Independence, which cut a deep division between Spanish-Americans and their mother country; and the other was the restoration of a harsh Spanish rule, which left no doubt as to the difference between them. There was also increasing friction between creoles and Portuguese, which compared with the experience of the earlier years, produced an entirely new situation in Brazil.

REPERCUS-
SION OF
EUROPEAN
EVENTS

When Ferdinand VII was restored to the throne of Spain after the Napoleonic invasion, there was much rejoicing both in Spain and in Spanish America. But the joy was short-lived. Ferdinand began by throwing out the Constitution of 1812 and ignoring its liberal advances; he also abolished the reforms of his grandfather, Charles III. The Jesuits were readmitted; titles were restored; and the Inquisition was reinstituted. Although these changes heralded a conservative reaction, the morality of the court and the morale of the country still remained low. Since the king trusted no one with ideas, only the most fawning adventurers rose. The fabric of Spanish society had been weakened by years of warfare and the fierce hatreds engendered by it. Insurrections and revolts were increasingly frequent. Authority inspired little respect. Political persecution became ever more intense.

In most of Spanish America the years of Ferdinand's absolute rule were generally unhappy ones. In Chile the Spanish military commander, exercising a despotic and arbitrary government, proceeded to punish the creoles, thus driving more and more of them into the camp of those who eventually were to reassert independence; and in Colombia the restored government executed five hundred patriots, including the scientist Francisco Caldas. The ports of Chile and Venezuela were again closed to all except Spanish trade. In Caracas, for example, British imports had amounted to over £85,000 in 1812, but fell to just over £5,000 in 1815.* Only in Mexico was the situation different. Ferdinand sent a new viceroy there in 1816; he decreed a general amnesty and restored the unity of the viceroyalty. The years of peace were a welcome respite from the horrible bloodshed and destruction of the preceding years. The more radical young creoles found no audience when they spoke of independence; the masses had been cowed by superior Spanish forces, and the wealthy creoles were reinforced in their conviction that Spanish rule spelled prosperity.

Then European events gave another spin to the wheel. During January 1820 in Cádiz a mutiny broke out within an army being prepared for the American theater. The mutiny became an insurrection, and Ferdinand was forced to restore the Constitution of 1812. The liberals were once again in control of Spain. However their hopes of winning back the loyalty of Spanish-Americans with liberal blandishments were doomed to failure. What the Spanish liberals failed to understand was that the ties between America and Spain had become frayed in 1808 when the Spanish throne was usurped; that many strands had been entirely broken in 1810 when the Central Junta disbanded, Spain appeared lost, and Spanish administrators failed to allow temporary self-rule in America; and that the remaining threads had been severed in 1815 when Ferdinand initiated

---

* Dorothy Burne Goebel, "British Trade to the Spanish Colonies, 1776–1823," *American Historical Review*, vol. XLIII (January 1938), 301.

his reactionary policies. Only massive force could have restored Spanish power in America, and then only temporarily; but the Spanish liberals lacked the will to use massive force even if they could have marshaled it.

Ferdinand's foreign allies restored the absolute monarchy to Spain in 1823, and they might well have tried to do the same in Spanish America, but the British, having succeeded at last in opening the ports to direct trade with northern Europe, were not about to allow them this opportunity. Aware of this British commitment, the United States rushed to issue the Monroe Doctrine, thus gaining credit for a policy that only England could enforce. Without reinforcements from Spain or her allies, the Spanish forces in Latin America were unable to hold out against the revolutionaries.

LEADERSHIP  Insurgent leadership during the Second War of Independence revealed marked contrasts as well as some similarities among the various countries of Latin America. Historians have traditionally attributed a great deal of importance to unique personalities, but it may be that it was not the individuals that produced the events but the other way around. Surely when similar events occur under differing leaders the importance of the person is at least thrown into question. A theory of revolutionary leadership cannot be developed here, but a few sketches may be useful before examining the events.

After Bolívar's flight from the chaos of Colombia in 1815, he remained undaunted and clear eyed. From his haven in Jamaica he wrote one of the most famous documents of Spanish-American history, in which he surveyed the origin and course of the revolution by region, analyzing the problems and prospects for the future, and then outlined his political philosophy, reasserting his commitment to establish freedom in South America. He believed that the people were unprepared for democratic procedures because the Spaniards had deprived them of governmental experience and that, therefore, a strong central government controlled by a powerful executive was the only alternative to anarchy. But it was not so much his writing as his *machismo* that gained him his leadership. The qualities of *machismo*—the ability to dominate, to impose one's will, to exercise charisma, to display the qualities of a stallion both in derring-do and in attracting women—were, and still are, much admired in Latin America. Bolívar had them all. His relationship with Manuela Sáenz, sometimes called *La Libertadora del Libertador,* will exemplify this trait. During a triumphal entry into Quito, Bolívar caught a wreath of flowers thrown from a balcony by a vivacious young woman. That night he met her at a ball, and from that moment on his fate was linked to hers. Manuela's nonconformist spirit was expressed in a letter to her English husband: "Do you think me less honored because he is my lover and not my husband? Ah, I do not live by the social preoccupations invented for mutual torment!" * When a dissident group tried to assassinate him several years later, Manuela held the assassins at bay with two pistols while Bolívar escaped through a window.

In Argentina another leader now rose. He was José de San Martín (1778–1850), the son of a Spanish civil servant. His family returned to Spain when the boy was young, and he entered the Spanish army at eleven, eventually rising to positions of responsibility. Disgusted with events in Spain, he left there and offered his services to the government of Buenos Aires in 1812, harboring a somewhat romantic attachment to the cause of independence. In Buenos Aires he became acquainted with the intellectuals, although he did not share with them their desire to transform the social structure. San Martín differed sharply from Bolívar. The Argentine was reserved and unemotional, even cold, and marital infidelity was never attributed to him. In his campaigns he relied on careful planning rather than on improvisation. He did not believe in modernization as did Bolívar, but limited himself to winning battles. He is not as great a soldier-statesman as Bolívar, but his virtues are nevertheless admirable.

In Mexico the new leader was Agustín de Iturbide (1783–1824), the son of a prosperous Basque immigrant. Iturbide was an officer in the creole militia when Hidalgo's

---

* Hubert Herring, *A History of Latin America from the Beginnings to the Present,* 2nd ed. (New York: Knopf, 1961), p. 268n.

revolt broke out. Despite Hidalgo's entreaties, Iturbide scorned the movement and devoted his energies to quelling the revolt. For his efforts he was made military commander of Guanajuato in 1813, and there proceeded forcefully to pacify the country. But his harsh means were inappropriate to the purposes of the new viceroy who was determined to win over the opposition and create an enduring peace, so he was removed from his command in 1816. Four years later, however, he was placed in charge of an expeditionary force to eradicate the last focus of subversive activity, the band of Vicente Guerrero. Instead of carrying out his orders, Iturbide struck a bargain with Guerrero and declared for independence, being careful to place himself at the head of the emerging new regime.

Instead of a colorful statesman like Bolívar or an austere military planner like San Martín, Mexico at this juncture had only the self-seeking Iturbide to lead it toward independence. Perhaps the deficiency of leadership was related to the bitterness of the earlier social protest, for it seems clear that a leader had to limit himself to only the goal of independence from Spain to be successful at that time. When a leader took on the ideals of radical social change, he was doomed to defeat. As the cause of independence was thus discredited, it became the device of later opportunists rather than the creation of heroic figures.

In Brazil two men together had the combined qualities of Bolívar: one was José Bonifácio de Andrada e Silva (1763–1838), known simply as José Bonifácio, and the other was the prince regent, later Emperor Pedro I.

José Bonifácio was born into a relatively wealthy family in São Paulo and was dispatched to Europe at an early age to complete his studies. He was greatly influenced by the Enlightenment, but like many European intellectuals, he was shocked by the excesses of the French Revolution and rather preferred "enlightened" England. After thirty years in Europe, he returned to Brazil and became Pedro's closest adviser in 1820. He persuaded Pedro to declare independence and played the chief role in the constitutional convention which Pedro summoned. Recognizing that power must be restrained and that the Brazilian people were not ready for an idealized republic, he sought the middle ground: a constitutional monarchy and restrictions on the power of the king. He believed these would preserve the monarchy. Although he was finally exiled two years later, he fully deserves the title "Patriarch of Independence." Bonifácio had the statesmanship of Bolívar.

Pedro had the *machismo* of Bolívar. He subdued opponents by a mere look and impressed a nation of horsemen with his horsemanship. Despite having had little formal education, he was competent at languages, quickly grasped the intricacies of constitutional structure, and immediately perceived political advantage. He liked to think of himself as a liberal, and indeed, was at ease with the masses, having been brought up among stable boys and palace servants, but he was an autocrat by temperament. At one time he cried, "Everything for the people but nothing by the people!" Like Bolívar, Pedro was deeply affected by an illicit love affair. He made his mistress a marchioness and allowed her to sit at meetings of the Council of State. Pedro and Bonifácio together provided the leadership for independence.

ARGENTINA AND URUGUAY
The restoration of Ferdinand VII created problems in Argentina, for it brought long-postponed issues to a head. The accepted myth of loyalty to a dispossessed king was no longer tenable now that he was firmly reinstalled upon his throne. Thus Argentina would have to submit to Spanish rule or to declare itself independent. If independence were to be declared, should the new nation be a monarchy or a republic? If a monarchy, who should rule? If a republic, should the government be centralized or federal? These questions could no longer be avoided and were the chief ones placed before the constituent congress that gathered at Tucumán in 1816.

The congress declared the independence of the United Provinces in South America in 1816, but beyond this it was unable to proceed because the conservative delegates, greatly influenced by the now prominent San Martín, desired a monarchy. In the meanwhile the congress appointed Juan Martín de Pueyrredón (1777–1850) as supreme director. He was a friend of San Martín, a monarchist, and a man of influence, having won fame in the battles against the British. Being a *porteño*, he was uneasy in the isolated vastness of the interior at Tucumán and soon persuaded congress to continue its proceedings in Buenos Aires. For the next three years congress deliberated while he directed a vain search for a king and became the government.

Pueyrredón believed, as did congress, that the new nation should include the territory that was formerly part of the Viceroyalty of the Río de la Plata. However, not only was Uruguay under the rule of Artigas, but also the caudillos in the five provinces immediately to the north of Buenos Aires owed their allegiance to the Uruguayan leader. If he failed to win back these provinces and incorporate them in the nation, he would lose even the confidence of those provinces that had chosen him supreme director. Just before Pueyrredón assumed his new post, the government of Buenos Aires had entered into negotiations with the Portuguese in Brazil, inviting them to invade Uruguay. When Pueyrredón took his new post, he encouraged these negotiations, for he saw in them the opportunity to gain control over the other areas under Artigas' influence.

The plan worked well in eliminating Artigas. The Portuguese armies invaded Uruguay in August 1816 and occupied Montevideo by January 1817. Artigas threw all his resources, both those in Uruguay and those from his allied provinces, against the invaders, but his forces were vastly overshadowed by the Portuguese armies. Still Artigas did not capitulate, but for three more years continued a guerrilla campaign against the Portuguese until he was forced to seek refuge in Paraguay. The Portuguese finally were in control of Uruguay, and its independence was not secured until 1828.

Pueyrredón did not fare well, however, for although Artigas was no longer a threat, the caudillos of the northern provinces continued to oppose him. These local leaders, who had emerged to power as a result of the breakdown of the old order, did not wish to bow once again to the hegemony of Buenos Aires and were also opposed to the conservative ideology of the monarchists. Allying themselves now with other caudillos of western Argentina, they unseated Pueyrredón in 1819 and plunged the nation into a ten-year period of recurring anarchy, which only ended when a caudillo, Juan Manuel de Rosas, came to power and forced the entrenched regionalist feeling to yield to centralized authority.

During the period of the Second War of Independence, the leaders in Argentina were less interested in legislative programs of modernization than before; nevertheless the country became more modern. The continuing disruption of society created an essentially modern condition of social flux and mobility, even in the west, and the power of the conservatives, who wished to maintain the old social structure, was undercut by the onslaught of rough cowboys. By 1820 the traditional society of fixed relationships was altered, and a monarchy would have been an anachronism. The modernizing groups in Buenos Aires, although unable to enforce their leadership on the country, could at least take comfort in that fact.

The groups who had been most interested in Europeanization were now overshadowed in importance. The urban intellectuals, recognizing that change would be more difficult than they had at first envisioned, apparently were willing temporarily to ignore Europeanization and other major reforms. The cattlemen had secured all they wanted when they were given the freedom to export directly to the markets of northern Europe. The merchants were now more concerned with making Buenos Aires the entrepôt for the entire country than with moving the process of Europeanization still farther. Faced with the preeminent question of where power would be located geographically and socially, all these groups were willing to postpone the issue of Europeanization, at least during the first few years after 1816.

VENEZUELA
AND
COLOMBIA

Bolívar returned from Jamaica in 1816 and began to liberate Venezuela. Two new developments ensured his military victories over the next years: foreign aid and the support of the *llaneros*. The United States recognized Bolivar's belligerency, thus making it legal for American privateers, operating under various Spanish-American flags, to sweep the seas of Spanish shipping and isolate the Spanish armies; and English merchants, anxious to invade Spanish colonies with their goods, lent Bolívar more than £1 million, part of which he used to contract unemployed English, Irish, and Scottish veterans of the Napoleonic wars. By the end of 1817 Bolívar with this new support defeated the Spanish in the eastern llanos.

About this time the *llaneros* had a new caudillo, José Antonio Páez (1790–1873). He came from a poor background and had been forced to flee to the llanos at the age of seventeen after having killed a man in his hometown, apparently in self-defense. The greenhorn, hardened by the rough conditions and tough campanions, gradually emerged as the leader of all the *llaneros*. At the end of January 1818 Páez met Bolívar and placed his followers under Bolívar's command. With the augmented forces, Bolívar had control of the western llanos within a year.

Although the war was not won in Venezuela and no attempt was made to take Caracas, Bolívar decided to push on into Colombia. Just when the llanos were supposedly impassable because of the rains and military activity should theoretically have been at a standstill, his forces began a six-hundred mile march from central Venezuela toward Colombia, wading in water up to the waist and swimming the horses. They marched from the steaming lowlands up the narrow passes of the eastern slope of the Andes to intense cold. They slept in snow, covered only with a ragged layer of cloth. At 12,000 feet many died from altitude sickness, and their horses perished from the lack of food. On the plains near Bogotá, Bolívar won a decisive victory over a Spanish army at the battle of Boyacá on August 5, 1819. Although this was not a battle involving many troops, it shattered Spanish morale. The viceroy in Bogotá fled ignominiously, and Bolívar marched along an open road into the viceregal capital to be welcomed by wildly cheering crowds.

Spanish reinforcements were prevented from leaving Spain by the liberal revolution of 1820, and Morillo, the Spanish field commander in northern South America, was instructed to strike a truce. This he did and then resigned; he could not continue to maintain a colonial government if the armies at home were not interested. After the truce expired, Bolívar proceeded to mop up Spanish entrenchments along the northern coast. By June 1822 he had established the independence of most of Colombia and all of Venezuela with the exception of two minor enclaves, which remained under Spanish control.

Bolívar declared a general amnesty for all opponents, trying now to build a nation. He summoned delegates to one congress for both Venezuela and Colombia, for he wanted to make this one country, Gran Colombia. The delegates set up a centralized government to administer all of Gran Colombia through medium-sized departments and elected Bolívar president, but he immediately sought a leave of absence in order to pursue the war to the south and left Santander, the vice-president, in charge. Bolívar realized that until the Spanish were driven out of Peru, independence was not assured anywhere in South America. However his first target was Ecuador, for he wanted to include this area in Gran Colombia. Successful battles, especially those led by his chief lieutenant, Antonio José de Sucre, were culminated by Bolívar's romantic entry into Quito in 1822.

Bolívar left behind him in Bogotá a government committed to modern change and Europeanization. Educational institutions were revamped to conform to British pedagogical ideas. The tax structure was redesigned in accordance with the latest economic theories. National courts with a uniform basis replaced the colonial judicial structure dependent on corporate and class divisions. Although the progress of these ideas was soon halted by political instability, turning back was now impossible.

CHILE,
PERU,
AND
BOLIVIA

When San Martín was placed in charge of the Argentine Army in 1814, he soon perceived, as Bolívar saw later, that until the Spanish forces were crushed in Peru, the newly independent Argentine provinces would never be safe. And he had a new plan for how to crush the Spanish forces. His plan was to cross the Andes into Chile at a point where the ranges were relatively narrow, move across Chile to the coast, and go from the coast by sea to Lima to occupy the seat of Spanish power right away. Mopping up the highlands would then be a relatively easy task.

For three years San Martín prepared for the execution of his plan with the greatest care and attention to every detail while gathering his strength in western Argentina. In mid-summer (January) of 1817 he crossed the Andes into Chile. His move was preceded by elaborate feinting devices, so the Spanish army was caught unprepared and suffered a swift defeat; then he marched unhampered upon Santiago. After another major battle the next year he was in complete control of the central valley of Chile. Chile was made an independent nation, and O'Higgins, who had joined him in Argentina, was placed in charge of a government oriented toward modernizing programs.

Two years elapsed before San Martín was ready for the next move. For this part of the plan he needed a navy and a naval commander. The flood of unemployed British military personnel to Latin America caused by Napoleon's defeat—one sidelight of the Europeanization of Latin America at this time—came to his aid. Few men in Europe had established a greater reputation for daring exploits than Lord Cochrane, the future Earl of Dundonald, and he was available for hire. San Martín sent an offer to Cochrane, who accepted. By 1820 all was ready. The ships were loaded with the army and set sail under Cochrane's command to the south of Lima.

By now news of the new liberal government in Spain had arrived in Peru. Liberal Spanish officers who had fought in the Peninsular War were dissatisfied with the lack of imaginative leadership demonstrated by the ultra-conservative viceroy. Encouraged by the revolution in Spain, these officers deposed the viceroy and replaced him with a liberal, an action speedily approved in Spain. The new viceroy tried to reach a modus vivendi with San Martín, but San Martín was determined on complete independence, and the negotiations came to naught. The viceroy and the Spanish army then fled to the interior of Peru, and the *cabildo* of Lima sued for peace. San Martín entered and occupied the city in July 1821.

San Martín's fatal flaw now became apparent: He would not undertake any operation until he was sure of success. The Spanish army in the interior easily outnumbered his, so he awaited developments. Cochrane, claiming back pay and ever an opportunist, departed with the war chest and sold his services to Brazil; and the army of Argentines and

Chileans became restless and demoralized by the enforced inactivity.

A year later San Martín met Bolívar at a secret inter-view at Guayaquil, Ecuador. What transpired is still un-clear, but San Martín decided to leave the field and allow Bolívar to complete what San Martín had started. Back in Buenos Aires, despite his great achievements, San Martín was spurned by the liberals because of his conservatism and by the conservatives for his failure to rescue Pueyrre-dón's government when it was overthrown in 1819. Dis-illusioned, the man who had freed all southern South Amer-ica retired to Europe, where many years later he suffered a lonely death.

Bolívar assumed control in Lima in September 1823 and took almost a year to consolidate his political power there before facing the Spanish army in the interior of Peru. During this time the viceroy was having trouble with the Spanish forces to the south. They were commanded by an archconservative general whose failure to receive recogni-tion had apparently unbalanced his mind. The general now threw off the authority of the viceroy and declared that the area under his control would be an absolutist monarchy ruled by Ferdinand VII. The viceroy, finding entreaties useless, was forced to dispatch a desperately needed portion of his troops southward to overpower the general. Thus only a part of the Spanish army met Bolívar's forces. Bolívar won a clear victory in the interior of Peru in August 1824, and his forces, commanded by Sucre, then went on to defeat the Spanish army in the final battle of Ayacucho in December. Sucre next marched southward to clean up the remaining Spanish garrisons. A new nation was created there in 1825 and named Bolivia in honor of Bolívar. Sucre became its first president and attempted, valiantly but unsuccessfully, to create a modern nation tied into the European economic system. Bolívar returned to faction-torn Lima to become chief executive of Peru and attempted to establish a stable government.

Meanwhile, factional bickering had broken out in Gran Colombia, and Bolívar soon returned there to try to main-tain national unity and stability. But the forces of region-alism overwhelmed him and tuberculosis sapped his energies. He died December 17, 1830, on his way into exile. Three months before his death, Venezuela and Ecuador both declared their independence and shattered Gran Colombia. Manuela Sáenz, now scorned by the women of Bogotá who had once sought her favor, lived out her days in poverty. If Bolívar died sorrowfully, he is now remembered as much for his unflagging devotion to the cause of independence and his perceptive political theories as for his military role as the liberator of Venezuela, Colombia, Ecuador, Peru, and Bolivia.

MEXICO    In Mexico the very forces of conservatism and traditionalism that stymied the earlier movement for independence now ushered it in, in reaction to European events. Perhaps in no other place in Spanish America did news of the revolution of 1820 in Spain have a greater influence. Mexican conservatives believed the world was divided between the liberals, whose wish to create modern secular states with individual freedom and mobility threatened all the conservatives held dear, and those like themselves, who believed every man had a fixed place according to his social status with God and king above all. Now the revolution in Spain had given new vitality to the liberal virus. Perhaps Mexico could still salvage the virtue of the Spanish heritage. If Ferdinand VII wished to escape the tyranny of his potentially regicidal subjects in Spain, he would be welcomed in Mexico in order to undergird the traditional social structure there. Meanwhile, Mexican liberals had come to the inescapable conclusion that without the support of the creole aristocracy independence was a pipe dream. If that support could be enlisted now, other modernizing reforms could be postponed.

The Second War of Independence in Mexico hardly deserves the name. When Iturbide was called upon to march against Guerrero both conservatives and liberals were ready for a change. As he moved closer to the rebel chieftain, Iturbide embarked upon an extensive correspondence with various factions in Mexico City and Veracruz. Out of that exchange of letters emerged a manifesto calling for three basic provisions: independence under a monarch, preferably Ferdinand VII; a guarantee of religion, which meant much more than an established church and symbolized the acceptance of the divinely ordained corporate society; and the end of any distinctions between creoles and Spaniards who joined the independent state. In this program there was something for everyone.

Iturbide struck a bargain with Guerrero, who joined the movement, and their joint forces set out for Mexico City. There were few battles to be fought toward that goal. In most places the potential opponents, led by creole militia officers, were beguiled by Iturbide's adroit use of propaganda and deserted to the revolutionaries. Sermons were preached denouncing the Spaniards and announcing that the war for independence was a religious war. Even the conservative city of Puebla, led by the bishop himself, joined the movement. Many Spanish soldiers in Mexico were as disheartened by the thought of a colonial war as were the troops that rebelled in Cádiz. When Iturbide promised them safe conduct back to Spain, they accepted it eagerly.

In July 1821 a new viceroy, Juan O'Donoju, landed in Veracruz, which along with Mexico City was one of the very few spots that had not joined the revolutionaries. In August O'Donoju signed a convention with Iturbide, agreeing to Mexican independence under the protective wing of Spain. A month later he entered Mexico City by Iturbide's side. They organized a provisional government, headed by a junta; O'Donoju had a seat in the junta and Iturbide was president. Spain refused to sanction the actions of O'Donoju, but there was little she could do about it, for only a couple of forts remained in Spanish hands. Mexico was at last independent.

BRAZIL  In Brazil the period from 1815 to 1820 was characterized by increasing friction between the creoles and the Portuguese. The presence of the king in Brazil solved old problems, but also created new ones. Fifteen thousand courtiers had flooded the small town of Rio de Janeiro just when the creole landowners found the city attractive for the first time. Many of the planters' town houses, rough-hewn though they were by European standards, were turned over to the courtiers; instead of gratitude, the courtiers evinced only spiteful and complaining scorn for the accommodations. Furthermore, the king gave all the best jobs in the administration to the Portuguese, which made a real point out of what had previously been a somewhat exaggerated rivalry between the creoles and Portuguese, and issued edicts and instructions on matters that the members of the *câmaras* had long considered their exclusive concern. The old Portuguese merchants were also displeased with the end of the colonial status, for now lesser creole merchants and foreign merchants, especially British ones, could compete with them openly and directly.

The presence of the king also exacerbated regional rivalries. Previously each province had thought of itself as one colony among equals; now Rio de Janeiro and the southern provinces loomed much larger than the northeastern provinces. The taxes that were collected by royal agents went not to finance Lisbon, but to develop the south. Thus the older northeastern provinces felt forgotten. The creoles in these provinces would have preferred that the king go back to Portugal and put all regions on an equal footing once again. When the king lingered on after Napoleon was expelled, resentment became more intense. Independence was no longer unthinkable because the king himself had made Brazil independent de facto and because the Spanish Americans, most notably Argentina, had now enjoyed it for some years. Then rumors swept the plantations that the king was considering abolishing slavery. In 1817 a short-lived abortive revolution broke out in the northeastern provinces with the aim of making the region independent as a republic. The movement presaged the coming struggle between centralists and federalists and between monarchists and republicans. The harshness with which the revolutionists were treated after their capture alienated still more creoles from the king.

In 1820 the liberals in Portugal, who were primarily the same Lisbon businessmen that were most hurt by the end of the colonial relationship, followed the example of Spain and revolted in behalf of a constitution. The king was to be circumscribed by a parliament, and he was to return to Portugal. King John now faced a difficult dilemma. If he did not return to Portugal, he would obviously lose that throne, for republican sentiment was not lacking there; if he did return to Portugal, he would probably lose Brazil, for the creoles were fiercely jealous of their new proximity to the king. His solution was a typically Portuguese one: compromise. He went to Portugal in 1821, but left his son Pedro as prince regent in Brazil with instructions, it is said, to make himself king if formal independence should come.

John was no sooner back in Lisbon than Parliament reduced Brazil to colonial status, limited Pedro's jurisdiction to southern Brazil, and sent out governors for the other provinces. Parliament was playing upon the known regional rivalries for its own advantage. Then it destroyed the courts and other national institutions that the king had created, and finally ordered Pedro home. The result was almost inevitable, given the thirteen years of independent status which Brazil had enjoyed. The Portuguese who surrounded Pedro urged him to obey the will of Parliament; the creoles insisted that he remain in Brazil. He acceded to the creoles' wishes in January 1822, thus defying the authority of the Parliament he had sworn to uphold. In June he summoned a congress to draw up guidelines for an independent nation, and in September he formally declared the independence of Brazil with himself as King Pedro I. The Portuguese were too weakened and too concerned with problems in Europe to dispatch troops to Brazil to combat the hastily organized Brazilian militia and navy, the latter under the supervision of Admiral Cochrane, just "retired" from Chilean service. The Brazilian forces besieged the Portuguese garrisons in Salvador and Belém, forced them to surrender, and dispatched them to Portugal.

Yet Brazil was still not truly independent. Pedro soon became dissatisfied with the deliberations of congress, which was devoting itself to xenophobic provisions designed to exclude all Portuguese from positions of power to compensate for the insults the creoles had suffered since 1808. Pedro took umbrage at the delegates' attitude and was irritated by their intractable behavior. He dissolved the congress and issued his own constitution, more conservative in tone than the draft congress had been discussing, but nevertheless maintaining many of the same provisions. His conservative constitution provoked immediate dissatisfaction among the creoles, and a new revolt broke out in Pernambuco. The rebellion was bloodily put down; little mercy was shown the defeated partisans. Pedro then surrounded himself with Portuguese advisers, which irritated the creoles even more; it was 1808 all over again!

John VI of Portugal died in 1826. Pedro was the rightful heir. Would he try to unite Brazil and Portugal once again? Or would he recognize that he could have neither throne without losing the other? This time, compromise did not work. Pedro abdicated the throne of Portugal to his daughter (born in Brazil) and arranged for her to marry his brother Miguel, who usurped the throne. Pedro was forced to fight for the rights of his daughter. Brazilian revenues were channeled into this dynastic quarrel, which seemed irrelevant and outdated to most creoles.

There were still other reasons for dissatisfaction with Pedro's rule. There was the sad defeat in Uruguay. After the success of the Portuguese armies in 1820, Uruguay had been given all the trappings of a Brazilian provincial government, but the real power resided in the army of occupation. Although a large part of the army of occupation departed for Portugal after Brazil became independent, the Brazilian contingent, that is, soldiers of whatever origin but loyal to Pedro I, was large enough to maintain Uruguay in Brazilian control. In 1825 thirty-three patriots of Uruguay invaded from Argentina, and local dissidents rose up in revolt to greet them. New juntas were formed that made a pretense of joining Argentina, which sent in armies to help. The Brazilians suffered repeated defeats until only Montevideo was in Brazilian hands two years later; Argentina controlled the rest. The British, whose trading interests were damaged by the warfare, then stepped in to moderate the quarrel and forced both contenders to grant Uruguay independence as a buffer state between them. Both the Argentine and the Brazilian governments lost prestige at home, and Pedro was discredited as a military leader. Also as a price for British diplomatic recognition, he agreed to end the slave trade by 1830. Legislation to that end was drafted, and tensions mounted. The creole landowners believed that the economic basis of the country would be destroyed and that they would be plunged into poverty if no more slaves could be brought in.

Since Pedro had declared independence, all his policies had turned the creoles against him. Finally, in April 1831 a mob was sufficiently stirred up to march on the palace; the creole militia had already been won over; there was no other choice for Pedro I but to give in. But the creoles also feared republican anarchy, so they forced Pedro to abdicate in the name of his five-year-old, Brazilian-born son. He could be brought up according to norms more suitable for this American empire, and he was to have as tutor José Bonifácio. Regents chosen by a Brazilian parliament would rule during the boy's minority. One point he would thoroughly absorb was that the creoles must be treated with the greatest circumspection. At last Brazil was being run by Brazilians. In this sense independence was only now complete in Brazil.

*　　*　　*

Although the independence movement in Brazil was markedly different from that of Spanish America, a comparison between the two areas reflects certain similarities. The key figures during the independence movement were the creole landowners and their desire for power impelled them increasingly to reject peninsular authority. During the First War of Independence the creoles had the experience of being ruled from a capital within their own borders, and after the war the behavior of Spanish and Portuguese administrators increased the tensions between themselves and the creoles. At some point in both areas creole militias found it useful to make a show of force. The British interest in opening up the ports played an important role in the independence movement, and both the Spanish and Portuguese merchants, who once monopolized international commerce, suffered thereby. The opening of the ports fostered the Europeanization of both areas. Finally, regional tensions rose in Brazil as in Argentina, Chile, Colombia, and Mexico.

A comparison between Brazil and Spanish America also indicates certain differences. Brazil maintained a legitimate government through the presence of a king accepted as the rightful heir to power by most elements in society; the entire Portuguese colonial area remained united despite regional friction; the traditional, corporate society survived; and the absence of warfare retained the old order. The principal explanation for all these differences is not national character, as sometimes alleged, but the purely accidental presence in Brazil of the king. Of course, there are other lesser factors that help explain these developments. If the king of Spain had come to America, it is doubtful that he could have maintained the allegiance of the entire Spanish colony; that is, there was apparently a greater preexisting unity in Brazil than in Spanish America. Also, the intellectuals of Brazil did not play as important a role in establishing political independence as the intellectuals did in Spanish America. The backwardness of education in Brazil explains this fact, as it does the subsequently lesser pressure toward modernization there. Brazil had never enjoyed the splendor and cosmopolitanism of Mexico City, nor was it in the process of developing a new economic frontier, as was Argentina. Finally, it would have taken an enormous crisis in Brazil to produce a social upheaval comparable to that in Mexico, despite the large mass of oppressed slaves in Brazil. Perhaps their very slavery and the consequently greater destruction of their psychological capacity to react explain this fact. On the other hand, if years of warfare had ravaged the countryside, upset old spatial and social relationships, and forced landowners to free and arm the slaves, it is conceivable that the result would have been more like that of other American nations. In any case, the comparative approach to the story of independence in Latin America suggests that there is more similarity between Brazil and Spanish America than usually thought, just as it implies that there is a greater difference among the nations of Spanish America.

# Chapter 9

# The Meaning of Independence

How significant were the changes wrought by the wars of independence? Bolívar concluded that he had "ploughed the seas," * and other participants probably felt the same disillusionment. Subsequent historians have sometimes similarly observed that the main problems Latin America faced in 1810—underdevelopment, lack of entrepreneurial spirit, arbitrary and unrepresentative government, ignorance, exploitation, social injustice—are the same ones it faces today and that nothing really has changed in the last century and a half, much less in those fifteen years of revolution. But to begin along a road is often as difficult a step as to traverse it. And many of the difficulties of Latin America today are basically problems of transition from the Spanish and Portuguese colonial systems; if this transition has been going on for so long, it is only because of the strength of preexisting institutions. The era of independence was of genuine significance in the history of Latin America.

EUROPEAN-IZATION  Independence fostered the integration of all Latin America into the new European system. The expanding forces of industrial capitalism, centered in England, succeeded in

---

* Gerhard Masur, *Simón Bolívar* (Albuquerque: University of New Mexico Press, 1948), p. 687.

penetrating the previously closed Spanish and Portuguese empires, and this change brought on social and intellectual changes as well. Imports from northern Europe and exports thereto multiplied rapidly. This kind of change concomitantly produced an expansion of plantation agriculture and cattle raising to supply the expanding needs produced by Old World manufacturing development and urbanization. The onslaught of cheap European manufactured goods simultaneously destroyed ancient craft industries in Latin America. Latin American cities began to look to northern Europe for models, and the rural-urban dichotomy became more intense. Moreover, new, more Europeanized centers emerged to prominence while old ones declined still further: Argentina and Chile became the dominant Spanish-speaking areas of South America, replacing Peru from a position it had long held and has never regained. The widening currents of European influence eroded away the walls of conservatism and traditionalism and opened up channels for the circulation of fresh forces. In summary, independence advanced processes begun in the eighteenth century, although regional variations continued to affect the rate of change.

The opening of the ports was the most concrete example of the new regimen. As a British businessman in Buenos Aires put it in the 1820s: "On a free trade being tolerated by the viceroy in 1808, it was at once seen that the country was in every respect fitted for great commercial improvement; and on being thrown open altogether in 1810, it was very soon carried to an extent altogether unknown in former times: for the barriers of exclusive privilege and monopoly being once thrown down, the commerce of the country advanced at a pace beyond all example." * In Brazil the value of British goods imported directly went from just a little over £1,000 in 1806 to over £2,000,000 in 1812 to over £3,000,000 in 1818; in Argentina it went from £369,000 in 1812 to £1,104,000 in 1824; in Mexico from £21,000 in 1819 to more than £1,000,000 in 1825;

---

* In R. A. Humphreys (ed.), *British Consular Reports on the Trade and Politics of Latin America, 1824–1826* (London: Royal Historical Society, 1940), pp. 31–32.

and in Chile from £37,000 in 1817 to £150,000 in 1819 to nearly £400,000 in 1822.

The hope of exporting vast quantities of Latin American produce to northern European markets was frustrated in many places by the damages inflicted by the war. British businessmen reported, for instance, that in Uruguay the "invasion by the Brazilians . . . completed the ruin which Artigas had begun. Accordingly these once flourishing provinces are now exceedingly poor; the immense herds which in former times covered their rich pasture grounds have entirely disappeared." * The civil disorders of Argentina produced a similar though less serious effect. The possibility of exporting from Chile to Europe had never been great, and exports continued to be principally mineral; that is, gold and silver the Chileans earned by trading with Peru and Bolivia. The exports from Peru were chiefly precious minerals, and, after the first rush to exchange accumulated supplies for newly cheap imports, gold and silver were in relatively short supply compared to colonial days because of the destruction of the mines. In Venezuela the events of the wars similarly resulted in abandoned estates or only partially cultivated plantations. On the other hand, such exports as were made were no longer funneled through a parasitic mother country. Whereas in 1820 practically all exports of Mexico were shipped to Spain, by 1823 only a tenth of its exports went there, and at least a half went directly to other parts of Europe or to the United States.

The new trading relationships with overseas nations deeply affected commercial patterns within Latin America as well. The British consul in Mexico reported that "formerly the principal and most opulent merchants of New Spain were established in the city of Veracruz. They were either old Spaniards or their immediate descendants." These merchants sold to wholesalers in Mexico City who distributed imported goods to retailers around the country. "Since 1810 nearly the whole of the opulent Spanish merchants have withdrawn their families and capital from New Spain. . . . The[se] individuals are, now, principally replaced from Great Britain, and as these are almost ex-

* *Ibid.*, p. 40.

clusively commission merchants they find it more advantageous to supply directly the retailers. They have therefore, all established themselves in the City of Mexico, having mere agents at the ports." * Similar alterations in channels and procedures doubtless occurred throughout the continent.

If we compare the foreign trade of the various parts of Latin America it becomes apparent that four factors affected the growth in the volume of exports and imports. First, and most important, was the presence or absence of resources suitable for introduction into the international economy. Second was the existence of a commercial structure adequate to exploit this potential, including, especially, merchants with sufficient capital and know-how. Third was the difficulty or ease of transporting raw materials to the European consuming centers and manufactured imports to the Latin American population. Fourth was the degree to which military operations had left the resources, the commercial structure, and the means of transportation unscathed. By any one of these measures, Brazil comes out ahead. Just at the time of independence, coffee began to be planted there on a large scale. Rich Portuguese merchants were gradually superseded by the British without any shock to the commercial system. Both the new coffee areas and the older sugar ones were near the coast, and independence had been won virtually without warfare. Thus one can see that although the Europeanization of Latin American economic life was a secular process principally impelled by changes occurring in the Old World, its specific effect depended upon the particular conditions in each part of Latin America. On the other hand, all of Latin America headed in the same direction, even if at a different pace.

Since independence Latin American governments have always been heavily dependent on foreign loans either because of their unwillingness to tax the major sources of internal wealth or because of government extravagance. The pattern was set during the Second War of Independence when the authorities sent agents to London to negotiate bond issues with bankers. The agents varied in effectiveness,

---

* *Ibid.*, pp. 302–303.

but eventually succeeded in raising several major loans. The Colombian agent sent by Bolívar, for instance, negotiated for £2 million in 1822. By 1825 Latin American governments had borrowed over £21 million in England, of which £7 million was for Mexico, £6.7 million for Colombia, £3.2 million for Brazil, £1.8 million for Peru, and £1 million for Chile. A large part of these loans was taken up in commissions and fees to the banks, and only some £12 million was actually netted from them for government expenditures. As the Latin American agents who negotiated them were not always wise in their use, even less than this sum actually reached Latin America. By 1827 every Latin American bond issue was in default, although Brazil resumed payments in 1829. It was not until the 1860s that British investors again showed any willingness to buy Latin American government bonds. Through this experience the relationships between Latin Americans and Britishers had become closer, though not necessarily more cordial.

Private investment followed trade, and foreign capital came to dominate the economy of Latin America. The news of the final defeat of Spanish armies in 1824 led London investors immediately to speculate in fly-by-night mining companies designed to exploit the fabled riches of Spanish America from Mexico to Bolivia. Some £3 million were invested in such ventures. But neither the welcoming governments nor the investing community was mature enough at that time to overcome the challenges presented by Latin American terrain, climate, backward transportation, and traditional attitudes. One company, the Potosí, La Paz and Peruvian Mining Association, sent out four representatives to initiate its operations. They consumed a large part of the company's initial capital of £50,000 in luxury provisions for their travels, including, according to a participant, "gingerbread nuts and peppermint drops." * The machinery, tools, quicksilver, furniture, supplies, and skilled workmen never even reached their Bolivian destination, and the agents, for lack of further funds from London, were

---

* Quoted by William Lofstrom, "Attempted Economic Reform and Innovation in Bolivia under Antonio José de Sucre, 1825–1828," *Hispanic American Historical Review*, 50 (1970), 293.

eventually forced to sell their clothing, watches, and jewelry to survive. Most such companies went bankrupt, but the precedent was set for later investments on a much larger scale that were to prove more successful.

Europeanization meant the erosion of the peculiarly Latin American modes of life insofar as the centers of culture there began to look increasingly to northern Europe for everything. For instance, many an exquisite, superbaroque architectural decoration had been chiseled away in the late eighteenth century to comply with European esthetic standards. It is difficult to find examples of Latin American art, architecture, or music dating from the first half of the nineteenth century that are as worthy of admiration as the colonial work. It was now all mere mimicry, and poor at that. Similarly, the clothing styles of the Europe-oriented cities varied according to Parisian fads or London customs. Even the furniture and the diets of the urban groups were affected. These forces were especially noticeable in the larger cities and thus served to further differentiate urban from rural life in Latin America.

Europeanization proceeded at an even faster pace after about mid-century once the international economy had settled down to patterns that were to characterize it until World War I. Impelled by technological developments, especially in transportation, the lifting of tariff barriers in Europe, the large-scale migration of European peoples, and the mobility of capital, Latin America was swept ever further into the European vortex. Although the years of political instability during the first half of the nineteenth century limited economic growth and disappointed many a British exporter, British exports to Latin America increased nevertheless and were to skyrocket once railroads extended the orbit of European commerce far beyond the ports. Massive investments in railroads, mining enterprises, urban services, cattle ranches, and other enterprises characterized the latter half of the century. The United States followed in England's footsteps. With these investments, of course, went power. Although to listen to the plaintive complaints of the investors their lot was one of constant harassment by hypernationalistic governments, the more common attitude among government officials was rather one of sycophantic pleading interspersed with sly acquisitive suggestions.

It is not surprising then that postindependence Latin American economies have often been labeled "neocolonial." It seemed as if the economic place of Spain was now held by England or, later, by the United States. The subsequent struggle to industrialize is therefore often considered still another war of independence. And since much of the early industrialization of Latin America was financed by foreign capital and directed by foreign management, so that every action of the governments to tax, restrain, or inspect these economic interests ran aground on the power of foreign governments, many Latin Americans today believe true independence requires industrialization under national control, carried on by the state if necessary.

MODERN-
IZATION

The transformation of Latin America initiated during the eighteenth century was greatly speeded up by the independence movement. Although the traditional society can hardly be said to have been destroyed, it was now under heavy attack. Its corporate structure was as threatened by the removal of the king as a family's cohesiveness is by the death of a father. The complex layering of craft guilds, church corporations, racial groups, and propertied classes was shaken up by these events and would never be the same. Political and economic liberalism opened the way for the individual to break out of the bonds of his social origin and rise—or sink—according to other criteria. Although not completed then or later, the process of modernization had been hastened.

The chief intellectual burden of the independence movement was liberalism—the release of the individual from the binding force of a static, stratified social structure. This liberalism was still chiefly informed by the Enlightenment, and the concept of natural rights was paramount within it. Latin American thinkers considered freedom of speech, the press, religion, and association basic to any governmental system. They believed constitutions were necessary to restrain the government and lay down the rules of the game for everyone, and the separation of powers would ensure their execution.

The failure fully to implement these reforms stemmed not so much from the alleged reluctance of the new leaders to impose strong government, but from their refusal to come to terms with the landowners and other privileged social groups they encountered—that is, with the forces of traditionalism. O'Higgins, for instance, was a strong executive who accepted the necessity of centralized power. He strengthened the police, captured bandits, encouraged trade, killed his opponents or sent them into exile, intervened in elections, and attempted to perpetuate himself in power. But he also abolished entail, attacked the church, ignored titles of nobility, and tried to break down the ancient barriers between the classes. That is why O'Higgins' regime was relatively short-lived. Other reformers met with similar failures: Rivadavia in Argentina, who attempted to strengthen the freedom of the individual; and Valentín Gómez Farías, president of Mexico from 1832 to 1834, who abolished state monopolies, ended the *fueros* of all corporate groups, revoked the compulsory payment of church tithes, and stripped the church of its educational responsibilities.

The major contribution of this generation was to elaborate a program and spell out its meaning in concrete acts. These men wished to expand educational facilities because only in this way would man's control over nature and society be possible. They tended almost invariably to separate church and state because their union was one of the major ways in which the hierarchical society was maintained.* They also identified the Spanish heritage as a bad one. It was, so they alleged, the chief cause of all their evils. If they were right, then they may be considered prophets of doom despite their optimism; for the Spanish heritage is all they had.

One should not exaggerate the degree to which Latin Americans copied standards of government from other

---

* By eliminating the king, the independence movement had already brought about this separation in thought if not in legal fact. Cut loose from this restraining force, the church in the nineteenth century was often as irresponsible in its actions as the army. European-driven change rather than stagnation lay behind these developments.

areas. In a provocative study, Professor Glen Dealy has recently shown the degree to which a Thomistic and colonially derived political theory was maintained in the early constitutions of Latin America.* John Locke's views and Anglo-Saxon political institutions were not as widely adopted in Latin America as is usually thought. The common good was not to be achieved by the satisfaction of conflicting interests and the balancing of powers, but through the morality of leaders. Uniform religious education, divine guidance, and control of speech and press were to be used to foster this morality. Many constitutions even embodied a board of censors to watch over the virtue of officials, and the constitutional qualifications for office sometimes included moral ones. Of course, in correcting one exaggeration one must not fall into another and suggest that the new political system cannot be differentiated from the old one.

The political theory of the time may also be studied in the thought of Bolívar. Deeply concerned with the nature of Spanish-American society, he was a political philosopher of no small importance. He always reiterated that "the excellence of a government is not in its theory, its form, or its mechanism, but in being appropriate to the nature and character of the nation to which it is applied." † Many of Bolívar's contemporaries believed that the rights of the individual could be best defended from the arbitrary action of the state if the central government were kept weak, the executive power curtailed, and state and local government exalted, whereas he believed in a powerful executive within a strong central government. Weak government, he thought, would lead to anarchy and anarchy to dictatorship; it was better to have a strong government to begin with, placed within the legal structure, than to end up with a strong government anyway, but under a tyrant. He recognized that the only alternative to the centralization estab-

---

* Glen Dealy, "Prolegomena on the Spanish American Political Tradition," *Hispanic American Historical Review*, 48 (1968), 37–58.

† Guillermo Morón, *A History of Venezuela*, John Street (ed. and tr.) (London: Allen & Unwin, 1964), p. 128.

lished by the Spanish crown was indefinite division. A strong executive, he said, would suit the Spanish-American experience, although a monarchy was out of the question, for the clock could not be turned back. Many of his ideas have now come to be commonplace in Latin America.

But despite these evidences of Latin American willingness to synthesize a new view of man with those inherited from Spain, the most important feature of the period was precisely the direction of the change. It was toward a conception of the individual as more important than his original status. Everywhere one finds the gradual replacement of the corporate judicial system by a uniform national court structure. And although individual freedoms were often curtailed, they were given a recognition never seen in colonial days.

The modernization of economic life was also characteristic of this era. The simplification of the tax structure is a good example of this. Instead of multiple rates on different articles of trade, monopoly contracts, Indian tributes, internal trade barriers, and special taxes to finance the operation of various corporations like the *consulado*, the tendency was now toward the creation of relatively uniform duties on imported goods. These levies were not intended as protective tariffs but as revenue-producing customs. The simultaneous but more gradual adoption of laissez-faire practices, that is, the removal of restrictions upon economic activity, was another result of the modernizing ideology of independence. Although today such practices have come to be identified with conservatism, in the context of the relatively static economy of previous times it was understandably hailed by those who wished to foster change during the early nineteenth century. They could not have been expected to know that when superimposed on the still remaining traditionalism, it would come to mean not only merciless exploitation but also opposition to development.

The Indians suffered under the new regime. Although steadily exploited for three hundred years, they had also been protected by the Spanish system. The Indians had had certain corporate rights, privileges, and exemptions that the new Latin American leaders sought to destroy. They felt that if the Indians were forced to sink or swim as a result of their own initiative and hard work, they would emerge from their subhuman condition, shake off their lethargy, and participate more fully in national life. But instead, the individualism of the new era exacerbated their exploitation by those better equipped for that kind of struggle.

On the other hand, outright slavery was now considered inimical to the interests of the state, as it restricted the free initiative of the individual. Outside Brazil the abolition of slavery was almost invariably one of the goals of the new leaders. In all of Spanish America except Peru, laws were adopted at the time of independence either abolishing slavery or providing for gradual emancipation. In fact, the war itself had greatly lessened the number of slaves, either by facilitating their escape or by offering them freedom in exchange for military service. Furthermore, colonial restrictions upon freedmen were now removed, and blacks and mulattoes were now on an equal legal footing with other citizens.

Although class divisions were by no means erased by the achievement of independence, there was a general blurring of distinctions. The so-called castes were no longer burdened with legal disabilities. Elaborate records regarding ancestry were no longer kept by the clergy—at least not in Mexico. The war itself had encouraged the rise of mestizos and mulattoes who had military talent. And since soldiers and officers were often paid off in land, a powerful symbol of status, many of them or their descendants entered the upper class. These tendencies were all more prominent in Spanish America than in Brazil. Again, preexisting variations or the differing course of events since 1810 can be adduced to explain these unequal results.

The increasing pace of modernization was also characteristic of the latter half of the nineteenth century under the leadership of a new generation. To begin with, these men were much more aware of the necessity of molding their liberalism to fit the reality rather than attempting to shape the latter by the former. In addition, economic conditions were changing so as to make some of the liberal programs acceptable to the rich. For instance, the transformation of Argentine agriculture now made it attractive to import immigrants to tend the prize beef herds, plant alfalfa, or raise wheat. Thus Domingo F. Sarmiento (1811–1888) was able during his tenure as president from 1868 to 1874 to institutionalize liberalism in Argentina. Its legitimacy now rested on the shared beliefs of the rural aristocracy and urban elite. In Chile, too, moving cautiously and slowly, the liberals were able to gain power and carry out many of their most cherished reforms in such a way as not to threaten the landed oligarchy. Even in Brazil large advances toward a modern society were made particularly as a result of the growth of a new export economy based on coffee and the identification of new landowners with the forces of change.

But in Mexico years of anarchy seem to have precluded the softening of the conservatives, and more forthright measures had to be taken. Liberals there, hardened by their earlier defeats, successfully waged a violent civil war lasting from 1858 to 1860 in order to impose their program. It included the end of corporatively held land, severe restriction of the church, and the final abolition of the *fueros*. When the conservatives turned to Napoleon III for support, offering the Mexican crown to French-supported Archduke Maximilian, they unwittingly placed upon the liberals the mantle of national heroism. When the French troops had to be recalled in 1867 to strengthen French defenses against Germany, the liberals quickly restored their power in Mexico.

But the liberal reforms continued to remove protective corporate institutions and expose the helpless to the raw competitive efforts of the better endowed. As the nineteenth century wore on, the mestizos and nonaristocratic middle elements of society tended to acquire enough power to move against the Indians in a feverish effort to milk from them the luxuries enjoyed less exploitatively by the upper classes. And the old creoles, rather than restraining the mestizos as Spaniards had once restrained creoles, seemed satisfied to divert the aggressiveness of the mestizos away from themselves.

In the twentieth century one may discern an attempted synthesis of the colonial heritage and the nineteenth-century promise. We have noted that industrialization has been advanced under close government supervision if not outright ownership reminiscent of Bourbon enlightened despotism or even Hapsburg royal monopoly. Sarmiento's easy willingness to admit the "inferiority" of the Spanish tradition was reversed by the self-conscious assertions of José Enrique Rodó (1872–1917), who, at the turn of this century, assured the youth of his native Uruguay that the Spanish heritage of spiritual, nonmaterialistic, transcendent values was worth more than a mess of industrialized Anglo-Saxon pottage. The surviving notion of a corporate society was given overt expression in the fascist-inspired constitutions of the nineteen-thirties as well as in the class representation of today's Mexican party system. The basic concepts of a corporate society underlie much of the ordinary Latin American's idea of government and the individual's relationship to it.

INSTABILITY
AND THE
CAUDILLO

Independence also meant the end of a government long considered legitimate in Spanish America. This result was perhaps the most obvious one, yet at the same time it was of the most profound significance. In fifteen years the insurgents swept aside a government that had ruled virtually unchallenged for three hundred. During all this earlier time there had been no coups d'état and no barracks revolts. Despite the latent anarchy which had characterized political life, the fact is that no one had seriously questioned the right of kings to rule or the right of the Bourbons to rule Spanish America. And as the head of a corporate society, the sovereign's continued reign ensured the legitimacy of the entire structure. When he was gone, society was decapitated.

The result was like that of removing the flywheel of a machine. Moving at a faster and faster speed, it began to break up; bolts, nuts, springs and gears flew in all directions. "This is chaos," wrote Bolívar. "Nothing can be done because the good people have disappeared and the bad ones have multiplied. . . . Everything is in a state of ferment and no men can be found for anything." * And, for a long time, in most countries of Spanish America rule by a dictator appeared to be the only alternative to anarchy. Forty revolutions occurred in Peru during the half century fol-

---

* Masur, *op. cit.*, p. 437.

lowing San Martín's arrival, and eight different governments ruled there during 1834 alone. From the death of Bolívar to the end of the nineteenth century, Colombia had an average of one revolution per year and one constitution per decade. The events in Argentina during the wars of independence have already made this point clear. The history of Mexico from 1821 to 1854 was dotted with revolts and coups d'état while constitutions were regularly written, ignored, and rewritten. The basis of legitimate government —the acceptance of its right to rule by most of the ruled— had been destroyed by the wars of independence.

In some countries, perhaps luckier than Mexico, the age of chaos was more quickly succeeded by the rise of a strongman, or caudillo. He was generally a military leader—either in the army or at the head of irregular forces—and he came to power by force and ruled as a dictator. But more than that, the caudillo exerted power through personal authority rather than through institutional means. He possessed charismatic qualities and could count on personal loyalties to maintain him in power.

The caudillo was (and is) the result of social transition and not the evidence of social stagnation. In a perceptive study Richard Morse has argued that there are marked points of comparison between the postindependence politics of Latin America and the Age of Despots during the Italian Renaissance.* In both cases a long established corporate society was seriously challenged. City-states or regions were carved out of a previously existing Christendom. Legitimate government was thus eliminated. The religious underpinnings of the old regime were thrown into question. Just as the papacy had then been just one among many temporal powers, the church now represented one of many competing forces, or, as a spokesman for Spain, a foreign, hostile power. Into this crisis of legitimacy stepped the Prince or the caudillo. Without claim to legal power, he asserted himself by his dynamism, his personalism, and his shrewdness. Like Savonarola, he may have been semimessianic in his appeal. In any case, he maintained his authority by guile

---

* Richard Morse, "Toward a Theory of Spanish American Government," *Journal of the History of Ideas*, 15 (1954), 71–93.

and cunning and, as Morse puts it, "by proving his strength in life." He was as unscrupulous regarding the attainment of power as Machiavelli could have wished, and sometimes as concerned for the welfare of his people as that writer urged.

The classic pattern of control by the caudillo involved the pyramid not just of power, but of loyalty, for there were usually many caudillos, one in each part of the country, yielding allegiance to a central one. At the bottom of the pyramid was the peasant; whoever controlled his loyalty, and it was generally the landowner, was worth the blandishments and attention of those who aspired to local political power, for even as the peasant worked, he held a weapon: the machete. The local caudillo in turn yielded his personal allegiance to someone he knew, and he who controlled the loyalty of all the other regional caudillos would rule the country. If no one controlled an overwhelming segment, the result was anarchy, instability, and civil war. Often, a subordinate became strong enough to challenge the chief. Then there was an inevitable struggle for power.

Another potential power base for the caudillo was the army. The wars of independence, of course, contributed directly to its importance. War served to glorify the military virtues, establish the sacred calling of the officer, give him the experience of command, and grant him a limited legitimacy as savior of his country. When the wars were over, generals wished to command nations. Signs of such a tendency can be seen in the figures of José Miguel Carrera and Bolívar.

The caudillo was not necessarily a landowner. Indeed, with notable exceptions such as Rosas, it was probably more characteristic for him to be a landless mestizo, dissatisfied with his position and anxious to rise. With land in the hands of the aristocrats, mines owned by foreign investors, commercial activity increasingly controlled by foreigners too, and industrial prospects still nonexistent, the quickest way to change one's status was to control the government. This had already become a pattern during the wars of independence. Páez, a man of humble background, was the major political figure of Venezuela until 1863.

If the caudillo rose by force, he generally fell by force, and, unless another caudillo was powerful enough to fill the breach, anarchy was the most usual outcome. Perhaps the only exception was Diego Portales (1797–1837) of Chile. Portales was no less a caudillo for being a successful businessman. He possessed both the qualities to attract loyalty and the strength of personality to enforce his will ruthlessly. He readily violated what the liberals called "individual rights"; exile or imprisonment was the fate of those who opposed him. In his private life he surrounded himself with gay blades and beautiful women, demonstrating another aspect of his *machismo*. But to these qualities he added those of the "perfect Prince." Not only was he genuinely concerned for the welfare of his country, but he managed to institutionalize his power in such a way that stability lived after him. His secret seems to have been to involve the oligarchy directly in power rather than allowing them to observe political antics from afar. The army, for instance, was virtually replaced by a militia commanded by the landowners themselves.

Order and progress were the catchwords of Portales' regime. His police put down brigands, enabling entrepreneurs to develop heretofore untouched mineral resources. And conservative intellectuals produced a new constitution which called for an exceedingly strong executive power. This, Portales felt, was in keeping with the nature of his country at this time. As he had earlier put it, his ideal republic would have "a strong centralizing Government, whose members are genuine examples of virtue and patriotism, and [who] thus set the citizens on the straight path of order and the virtues." * According to this constitution, intendants were to carry out the president's will in the provinces, and the suspension of constitutional guarantees could be decreed by the president at almost any time. Although Portales was skeptical of paper constitutions, these ideas clearly reflected his views on ideal government. Eventually liberalism and democracy might have their place,

---

* Simon Collier, *Ideas and Politics of Chilean Independence: 1808–1833* (Cambridge, Eng.: Cambridge University Press, 1967), p. 339.

but for now, discipline and hierarchy were preferred. He restored the previously abolished entailed estates and raised property qualifications for voting. Portales held the common man in contempt and believed only the activity of irresponsible demagogues would destroy public tranquility. Consequently, freedom of speech and press were curtailed. The end of the Spanish Empire had thus meant the end of a legitimate order that could be reconstructed only by returning, at least for the moment, to the hierarchical qualities of the colonial society, carefully entwining the interests of the state with those of the creole oligarchy.

Such a painful search for legitimacy was almost unnecessary in Brazil, where the Braganza dynasty remained in power. Once a wing of that dynasty accepted its "Brazilianness" and came to terms with the creoles, instability was eliminated, and no caudillo found a vacuum of power in which to move. When, in 1831, Pedro I abdicated in behalf of his five-year-old son, Parliament chose regents to rule in his behalf. But this was as close as Brazil came in those years to republicanism. Even so, the centrifugal forces of regionalism and the breakdown of authority were so great that the boy was hastily crowned as soon as he turned fifteen. Subsequently, the regime preserved many of the characteristics of the corporate, hierarchical society in which the landed oligarchy found full opportunity to express its political will. So, if no caudillos emerged there, it was because Brazil refused to enter the transitional era in which old structures are violently broken up. When a brief period of *caudillismo* followed the overthrow of the emperor in 1889, the coffee planters organized their own militia and replaced army officers with one of their own representatives, thus imitating in their own way the example of Chile.

If the crown in Brazil preserved legitimacy, it also prevented the pervasive regionalism of Latin America from forcing the creation of several nation-states. We have already noted the revolutions of 1817 and 1824 in northeastern Brazil, which proposed to create independent republics there. But the loyalty the crown inspired in most Brazilians enabled the central government to put down these revolts and others that broke out before the new king was firmly in control. After 1849 Brazil enjoyed forty years of political stability. So it remained one country despite its distinct regions and immense size.

The rest of Latin America, lacking a king to secure the loyalties of diverse peoples, broke into many nations. The Viceroyalty of Río de la Plata became Uruguay, Paraguay, Argentina, and Bolivia; Gran Colombia became Colombia, Venezuela, and Ecuador; and the Viceroyalty of New Spain first became Mexico and the United Provinces of Central America, and then fragmented into six separate countries. The regional struggles that characterized the era of independence in Argentina were not put to rest until the high-minded caudillo Justo José de Urquiza managed, in 1862, to find a solution through compromise for divergent regional interests. Chile probably had the most homogeneous society and the least divergent regions of any area in Spanish America, and yet it was also characterized by local rivalries that only strong government could keep in check. Likewise, the raging argument between federalists and centralists threatened at times to tear Mexico apart. Although a federal constitution was obviously a foreign import, the realities of Spanish America demanded some way of taking these divergent forces into account.

*     *     *

So, if we ask: What were the results of the expansion of Europe? What were the effects in Latin America of the new Europe-directed economic system, the new Europe-minted ideology, and the new Europe-modeled style of life? the answers are anarchy, regionalism, and the rise of the caudillo. Modernization and Europeanization were the principal causes of these developments, although, to be sure, the pre-existing conditions also explain them.

And, if these forces destroyed the bases of political stability, only new sources of governmental legitimacy can restore them. Given the circumstances of today, it may be that only the pursuit of nationalism and social justice—two ideas also, ironically, imported from Europe—will provide Latin American governments the same degree of legitimacy as that enjoyed by the king in that older corporate society. Yet if Europeanization some day no longer means maintaining Latin America on the periphery of decision-making process but comes to include genuine self-determination and real independence; and if modernization can eventually signify the fulfillment of man's potential not so much through the freedom of the individual to struggle but principally through his ability to cooperate and participate in the community, then the processes of Europeanization and modernization may be considered not only a major cause of Latin American difficulties, but also the chief promise of its future peace and well-being.

# Bibliography

Listed below are English books that I believe will be most useful to the reader interested in initiating a further study of the political independence of Latin America. Although the list is highly selective, there is a marked unevenness in quality among the books included because I have attempted to mention at least one on each major region. Thus, for Brazil a work by John Armitage published almost 150 years ago must be included because nothing else exists that is even worthy of mention. The biography of San Martín by Ricardo Rojas is overly eulogistic, but there is no other in English. Bolívar, on the contrary, has been studied by perceptive historians: Gerhard Masur's biography is excellent, although David Bushnell's collection of essays is perhaps even more useful for the beginner. Nor does quantity bear much relationship to quality. There is little as yet available in English on Chilean independence, but the book by Simon Collier is first-rate. Some of the best works have been those that have examined the relationship of non-Latin American countries to the movement there; I have in mind especially William Kaufman's diplomatic study and R. H. Humphreys' biography of Paroissien. William S. Robertson's *Rise of the Spanish American Republics* and Irene Nicholson's *The Liberators* are general accounts that stress the role of key individuals. They are lacking in interpretive power and are chiefly useful as chronological summaries. As for background reading, there is no better place to begin than with Charles Gibson's *Spain in America*.

Background

Carr, Raymond. *Spain, 1808–1939.* Oxford: Clarendon Press, 1966.

* Gibson, Charles. *Spain in America.* New York: Harper, 1966.

---

* Available in paperback.

Herr, Richard. *The Eighteenth-Century Revolution in Spain*. Princeton, N.J.: Princeton University Press, 1958.

Lanning, John Tate. *The Eighteenth-Century Enlightenment in the University of San Carlos de Guatemala*. Ithaca, N.Y.: Cornell University Press, 1956.

Lynch, John. *Spanish Colonial Administration, 1782–1810: The Intendant System in the Viceroyalty of the Río de la Plata*. University of London Historical Studies, 5. London: Athlone Press, 1958.

* Prado Júnior, Caio. *The Colonial Background of Modern Brazil*. Suzette Macedo (tr.). Berkeley and Los Angeles: University of California Press, 1967.

Whitaker, Arthur P. (ed.). *Latin America and the Enlightenment*. 2d ed. Ithaca, N.Y.: Great Seal Books, 1961.

General

Griffin, Charles C. "Economic and Social Aspects of the Era of Spanish-American Independence," *Hispanic American Historical Review*, Vol. XXIX (1949), pp. 170–187.

Humphreys, R. A. "Economic Aspects of the Fall of the Spanish American Empire," *Revista de historia de América*, No. 30 (December 1950), pp. 450–456.

* ———— and John Lynch (eds.). *The Origins of the Latin American Revolutions, 1808–1826*. New York: Knopf, 1965.

Nicholson, Irene. *The Liberators*. London: Faber and Faber, 1969.

Robertson, William Spence. *Rise of the Spanish American Republics as Told in the Lives of their Liberators*. New York and London: Appleton-Century, 1918.

Whitaker, Arthur P. "Causes of Spanish American Wars of Independence: Economic Factors," *Journal of Inter-American Studies*, Vol. II (1960), pp. 132–139.

Gran Colombia

Belaunde, Víctor Andrés. *Bolívar and the Political Thought of the Spanish American Revolution*. Baltimore, Md.: Johns Hopkins University Press, 1938.

* Bushnell, David (ed.). *The Liberator, Simón Bolívar: Man and Image*. New York: Knopf, 1970.

* Johnson, John J., and Doris M. Ladd. *Simón Bolívar and*

*Spanish American Independence, 1783–1830.* Princeton, N.J.: Van Nostrand, 1968.

Masur, Gerhard. *Simón Bolívar.* 2d rev. ed. Albuquerque: University of New Mexico Press, 1969.

* Trend, J. B. *Bolívar and the Independence of Spanish America.* London: Hodder and Soughton, 1946.

Mexico

Benson, Nettie Lee (ed.). *Mexico and the Spanish Cortes, 1810–1822: Eight Essays.* Austin, Texas: University of Texas Press for the Institute of Latin American Studies, 1966.

Hamill, Hugh M., Jr. *The Hidalgo Revolt, Prelude to Mexican Independence.* Gainesville: University of Florida Press, 1966.

Robertson, William Spence. *Iturbide of Mexico.* Durham, N.C.: Duke University Press, 1952.

Robertson, William Spence. *The Life of Miranda.* 2 vols. Chapel Hill: University of North Carolina Press, 1929.

Timmons, Wilbert H. *Morelos: Priest, Soldier, Statesman of Mexico.* El Paso: Texas Western College Press, 1963.

Southern Spanish America and Brazil

Armitage, John. *The History of Brazil, from the Period of the Arrival of the Braganza Family in 1808, to the Abdication of Don Pedro the First in 1831.* 2 vols. London: Smith, Elder, 1836.

Arnade, Charles W. *The Emergence of the Republic of Bolivia.* Gainesville: University of Florida Press, 1957.

Collier, Simon. *Ideas and Politics of Chilean Independence, 1808–1833.* Cambridge: Cambridge University Press, 1967.

Rojas, Ricardo. *San Martín, Knight of the Andes.* Herschell Brichell and Carlos Videla (trs.). Garden City, N.Y.: Doubleday, Doran, 1945.

* Romero, José Luis. *A History of Argentine Political Thought.* Thomas F. McGann (tr.). Stanford, Cal.: Stanford University Press, 1963.

Street, John. *Artigas and the Emancipation of Uruguay.* Cambridge: Cambridge University Press, 1959.

Foreign Influences

Griffin, Charles C. *The United States and the Disruption of the Spanish Empire, 1810–1822: A Study of the Rela-*

*tions of the United States with Spain and with the Rebel Spanish Colonies.* New York: Columbia University Press, 1937.

Humphreys, R. A. *Liberation in South America, 1806–1827: The Career of James Paroissien.* London: Athlone Press, 1952.

Kaufman, William W. *British Policy and the Independence of Latin America, 1804–1828.* Yale Historical Publications Miscellany, 52. New Haven, Conn.: Yale University Press, 1951.

Manchester, Alan K. *British Preëminence in Brazil, its Rise and Decline: a Study in European Expansion.* Chapel Hill: University of North Carolina Press, 1933.

Robertson, William Spence. *France and Latin American Independence.* 1939. Reprint. New York: Octagon Books, 1967.

* Whitaker, Arthur P. *The United States and the Independence of Latin America, 1800–1830.* Baltimore, Md.: Johns Hopkins University Press, 1941.

# Chronology

| | |
|---|---|
| 1700 | Bourbons replace the Hapsburgs on throne of Spain |
| 1776 | Viceroyalty of Río de la Plata established; commandancy-general created in northern Mexico |
| 1778 | Decree of Free Trade ends system of monopoly ports in Spanish America |
| 1780–1781 | Rebellion of Tupac Amaru in Peru defeated |
| 1789 | Portuguese crush conspiracy for independence in Brazil |
| 1806 | Miranda attempts to free Venezuela; first British defeat in Buenos Aires |
| 1807 | Second British defeat in Buenos Aires; Napoleon invades Portugal; Portuguese court and government sail for Brazil |
| 1808 | Brazilian ports opened to British trade; Joseph Bonaparte usurps Spanish throne; Central Junta of Seville coordinates anti-French effort; Montevideo organizes junta loyal to Central Junta; Mexican viceroy attempts revolution |
| 1809 | Juntas formed in Bolivia and Ecuador are crushed |
| January 1810 | Central Junta defeated and replaced by regency |
| April 1810 | Venezuelan junta assumes power and deposes captain-general |
| May 1810* | Junta replaces viceroy in Argentina |
| July 1810* | Junta assumes power in Paraguay |
| July 1810 | Junta takes over in Colombia |
| September 1810 | Hidalgo launches revolt in Mexico; junta organizes government in Chile |
| 1811 | Venezuelan congress declares independence; Hidalgo captured and executed in Mexico; Carrera leads coup in Chile, closing national assembly; triumvirate named in Buenos Aires; United Provinces of New Granada founded; Artigas retreats from Uruguay under threat of Portuguese invasion |
| 1812 | Spanish constitution promulgated; Spanish forces crush first independence movement in Venezuela |
| 1813 | British army and Spanish guerrillas drive French from Spain; Artigas reinvades Uruguay |

* Dates when countries became finally independent of Spain.

| | |
|---|---|
| 1814 | Ferdinand VII restored to throne of Spain; insurgents occupy Montevideo; Spanish forces victorious in Chile |
| 1815 | Spanish capture and execute Morelos in Mexico; Bolívar pens Jamaica letter outlining his political philosophy |
| 1816 | Spanish occupy Bogotá; Congress of Tucumán convenes in Argentina; new viceroy arrives to pacify Mexico |
| 1818 | San Martín decisively defeats Spanish forces in Chile |
| 1819 | Bolívar victorious at Boyacá |
| 1820 | Liberals revolt in Spain and Portugal; Iturbide unifies independence forces in Mexico with the Three Guarantees |
| April 1821 | John VI leaves Brazil in hands of son, Pedro, and returns to Portugal |
| July 1821 | San Martín takes over in Lima |
| August 1821* | Mexico becomes independent |
| July 1822* | Bolívar establishes independent Gran Colombia and decrees formal incorporation of Ecuador |
| September 1822* | Pedro I declares Brazil an independent empire |
| 1823 | Portuguese forces completely driven out of Brazil |
| 1824* | Battle of Ayacucho frees Peru |
| 1825* | General Sucre liberates Bolivia |
| 1828* | Uruguay wins independence from Brazil |
| 1830 | Bolívar dies; Gran Colombia breaks up into Ecuador, Colombia, and Venezuela |
| 1831 | Pedro I abdicates throne of Brazil to his infant, Brazilian-born son |

# Glossary

| | |
|---|---|
| *audiencia* | A high council to the viceroy and a court of appeals in Spanish America. |
| *cabildo* | A municipal or county council in Spanish America. |
| *cabildo abierto* | An emergency meeting of leading townspeople to discuss measures to be taken at a time of crisis. |
| *câmara* | A municipal or county council in Portuguese America. |
| *caudillismo* | The caudillo institution or practice of having caudillos. |
| caudillo | A leader of regular or irregular military forces who comes to power through a mixture of force and charisma and rules absolutely, usually until violently overthrown. |
| conquistador | A sixteenth-century Spanish conqueror of Indian civilizations. |
| *consulado* | A merchant guild. |
| Cortes | The Spanish and Portuguese parliaments. |
| creole | A person born in Spanish America of European descent who is, at least theoretically, free of Indian or Negro blood. In this book the word is also used for a person born in Portuguese America. |
| entail | The legal practice of settling property inalienably on a person and his descendants. |
| *fueros* | The special rights and privileges, especially to a separate court, pertaining to guilds, the Church, military officers, and other groups defined by occupation or class. |
| gaucho | A cowboy in southern South America, usually of mixed racial background and irregular habits. |
| hacienda | A large landed estate. The word is used in this book to signify more particularly the economically self-sufficient units that satisfied local rather than European demands for agricultural products and were characterized by social relations of authority-dependency between owner and worker. |
| intendant | A government administrator of a large area who reported on some matters directly to the king. In the eighteenth century he gradually replaced a complex system of regional and local agents. |
| junta | Any board or committee. In this book most often used to |

denote the committees set up to replace royal officials at the beginning of the independence movements.

*llanero*    A cowboy on the llanos of Venezuela, usually of mixed racial background and irregular habits.

llano    A plain, especially in Venezuela and Mexico, usually characterized by a cattle-raising economy.

mestizo    A person of mixed Indian and white ancestry.

mulatto    A person of mixed Negro and white ancestry.

pampas    The plains, especially in southern South America.

*pardo*    A person of mixed racial ancestry.

peon    A debt-slave on an hacienda.

plantation    A large landed estate. The word is used in this book to signify the economic unit that produced export crops for European consumption and were worked by black slaves or workers paid in cash who were only impersonally related to the owner.

*porteño*    An inhabitant of the port city of Buenos Aires.

viceroy    A direct representative in America of the Spanish or Portuguese kings, who was the highest executive, legislative, and judicial officer in each viceroyalty.

# Index

The text of this book was set on the Linotype
in Garamond, a modern rendering of the type
first cut by Claude Garamond (1510–1561). Garamond was a pupil of Geoffroy Troy and is
believed to have based his letters on the Venetian
models, although he introduced a number of important differences, and it is to him we owe the
letter which we know as old-style. He gave to
his letters a certain elegance and a feeling of
movement that won for their creator an immediate
reputation and the patronage of Francis I of
France.

Composed, printed, and bound by The Colonial
Press Inc., Clinton, Massachusetts.